Women Strikers Occupy
Chain Store, Win Big

Published in 2012 by
Haymarket Books
P.O. Box 180165
Chicago, IL 60618
www.haymarketbooks.org

ISBN: 978-1-60846-245-2

Distributed to the trade in the US through Consortium Book Sales and
Distribution (www.cbsd.com) and internationally through Ingram
Publisher Services International (www.ingramcontent.com).

This book was published with the generous support of Lannan
Foundation and Wallace Action Fund.

Book design by Eric Kerl.

Printed in the United States.

Entered into digital printing May 2019.

Women Strikers Occupy Chain Store, Win Big

The 1937 Woolworth's Sit-Down

Dana Frank

Haymarket Books
Chicago, Illinois

Contents

Interview
with Dana Frank

Conducted by Todd Chretien
December 12, 2011

Todd Chretien: I'd like to ask you about the parallels between the Occupy Wall Street protests and the great workplace occupations carried out by workers in the 1930s in their fight for union rights. So to begin with, Dana, can you speak about the precursors that led up to the occupation at Woolworth's? How did working people respond to the Great Depression? What were the movements, the strikes, the organizations that laid the basis for this type of action?

Dana Frank: Let's remember exactly when this strike happened: right in the middle of the Great Depression. The U.S. economy was a total disaster since 1929. At the worst point a third of the country was unemployed and another third was underemployed. But at the same time, by 1937 when the Woolworth's strike happened, people had a huge sense of hope because of the New Deal. The government of Franklin Delano Roosevelt had created all sorts of social programs to redistribute wealth and try to address the economic crisis. But let's be clear: the New Deal only happened because ordinary people were taking things into their own hands with huge social protests throughout the 1930s, and that's what got us the welfare state. We tend to think that people just roll over dead when things are terrible economically, but in reality it's just the opposite.

The most spectacular of those social movements in the thirties was the uprising of the labor movement through the Congress of Industrial Organizations, the CIO. It organized literally millions of people. That's when we got most of the big industrial unions that we take for granted, like the auto workers, steel, tire, electrical manufacturing. All of that was happening in 1936 and 1937. The most famous moment was when the auto workers sat down and occupied a General Motors plant in Flint, Michigan, for almost two months. And they beat General Motors cold. There was almost no union in there before, and they won union recognition, wage increases, and then, eventually, better and better contracts at GM.

So, in that winter of December 1936 and January 1937, the General Motors strike was going on in Flint, next door to Detroit, and it was really an astonishing thing. It was all over the headlines in the United States and all over the world for that matter, because GM was the biggest corporation in the world, and the workers completely defeated it. That victory then inspired people to all kinds of labor activism. People said, "Wow, if they can beat General Motors, anything can happen!" In fact, U.S. Steel, really soon after that, gave in to the Steel Workers Organizing Committee without a strike because it was so afraid the same thing would happen to it, too.

The Woolworth struggle was at this exact moment. These women said, "Whoa!" It wasn't just them, either. Two or three weeks after the autoworkers won, all these little strikes started breaking out in Detroit and all over the Northeast and upper Midwest, led by workers in laundries, in restaurants, in golf ball factories. They saw that the iron was hot, that there was a window of opportunity for activism. Public opinion was on the side of the General Motors strikers. Public opinion was saying, "Wait a minute, something is very wrong in this country. The wealth is completely out of kilter in this country in terms of who's rich and who's poor." Remember, General Motors was a sit-down strike, so the strikers had to have the moral authority and legitimacy to occupy private property and win. You can only do these things when people in the general public are feeling like, "They have a right to do this." That winter and spring of 1937 was an incredible, historic moment in U.S. history.

Could you say a few things about this question of seizing or occupying private property? As we know, private property is written into our constitution, it is sacrosanct, and unions have traditionally picketed outside workplaces, workers have withdrawn their labor from companies and corporations as the primary means of taking strike action. So how and why did workers decide to move their strikes inside?

It's important to underscore that these sit-down strikers were not trying to take property away from the owners. They were using a sit-down as a tactic while they were striking. Traditional strikes set up a picket line as big as possible around the workplace and the workers use that to prevent the employers from bringing in scabs. In a sit-down strike, you are already in there so they can't bring in scabs. Also, you have a sense of camaraderie and spirit and creativity, because what are you going to do in there all day, right? But because it's on somebody else's property, there are these questions of legitimacy. When people have a sense that the corporation, or whatever the target might be, is itself illegitimate, that it's obtained its power and wealth illegitimately, then you can have public opinion on your side. But I do want to emphasize that the strikers were not saying take the store away from Woolworth's. They were saying, "Give us just wages, shorter hours, don't make us pay for our uniforms." In terms of demands, they were not saying that "we should own it." Also, they were super, super careful to never damage a thing inside the store while they were in there.

But the Woolworth's strike *was* about saying, we are going to take our bodies and we are going to put them here and we are going to make some claims. That's what the Republic Windows and Doors workers did in 2008 in Chicago when they occupied their plant and said, "Wait a minute, you can't just shut down this factory without paying us." They were working with the United Electrical Workers' union, and they won, too. So, the sit-down is a tactic, it's about people thinking creatively about what it means to occupy something. Notions of property can shift during moments of fundamental economic crisis, such as the one we're in now. When the system isn't working, people start rethinking it; they challenge what's just and what's not.

Let's talk about these different types of occupations. In the 1930s, workers occupied their own workplaces, which gave them a certain legitimacy, camaraderie, as you said, but in the 1960s the occupations were by customers, African Americans who challenged segregation by demanding to be served at Woolworth lunch counters. They put their bodies on the line to take that space. Now, we see Occupy Wall Street and yet another type of occupation. As we speak, the West Coast ports are being blockaded, not by longshore workers alone, but by community members, youth, students, unemployed, and activists from other unions all in solidarity with rank-and-file longshore workers, and with the active support of some of those workers, but without the official recognition of the ILWU. So, what we see is a continuum of types of occupations. There's been a lot of talk in the mainstream press about how these new occupations are not legitimate because they are not being carried out exclusively by employees from those workplaces. So, two questions. First, in the 1930s, what was the attitude of the mainstream press and employers to sit-down strikes and, second, how do the past occupations, be they in the 1930s or 1960s, relate to what is happening today?

In the 1960s, the protests were about the rights of African American people to be served at Woolworth's lunch counters, so they were really about customers protesting racism in consumption. Whereas in 1937, it was about the exploitation of the Woolworth workers. But these issues are not separate, right? Those same people who couldn't get served at Woolworth's also couldn't get hired. Woolworth's in 1937 would only hire white workers almost entirely. And if African American people did maybe get hired—one or two men in the stockroom, or a woman cleaning up—they would be exploited even more than the white workers.

As for today, the most obvious parallel is Walmart. Walmart is one of the biggest forces in the world driving down labor costs and working conditions, not just in its stores but equally importantly in the factories that supply it, all over the world. That's why its products are so cheap. It creates poverty all around the globe, and then turns around and sells those products to other poor people whose poverty it has helped create, and rakes in the money. I mean, here's Walmart. It has 1.4 million workers in the United States and 2.4 million around the world—and that's not counting the tens, perhaps hundreds of millions of workers who manufacture the products it sells. It creates enormous wealth for the Walton family and other stockholders. Listen to this statistic: in 2007, the combined wealth of the six Walmart heirs was bigger than that of the entire poorest thirty percent of the United States' population. That is huge! These six people have more wealth than the entire bottom third of the United States! I think those types of numbers make people realize that something is fundamentally wrong. And WalMart is just the tip of a global iceberg of corporate-generated wealth; it's just one example.

So, what are you going to do about it? What's awesome about the Woolworth story—and you can see this in some parts of Occupy Wall Street—is that these young women were absolutely ordinary young people, they did not have a history of activism. They saw what their brothers and boyfriends and family members had done at General Motors and they said, "Hey, we can do that too!" They believed in themselves. They knew that the iron was hot, but they also had a sense of "We can do this, just by ourselves." They did have major help with allies in the labor movement, but it was their idea. They also knew how to sustain themselves emotionally because it was scary to be occupying a chain store in the middle of the night. The police could have blasted in at any moment. It was their bravery and their sense that enough is enough and we can take on Woolworth's and win. And that spread all over the city and country. This wasn't just about one group of women in one store. It spread to another store in Detroit. It spread to fifteen stores in New York City and it spread to all kinds of other stores around the U.S. It was about people believing that organizing works. And, of course, the big point of the story is that, amazingly, organizing did work. It was a complete victory.

They were also very smart and creative about running it themselves inside the store, for the most part. The initiative came from below, and I think there's a lesson there about successful organizing. There's a major lesson at the end of the strike, too. It was initiated and led by women, but they were cut out of the negotiation process at the end by the male union officials who came in to strike the deal with the company. So, what did that mean in terms of what we would now call union democracy and the internal democratic process of the movement? One of the things that's been beautiful about Occupy Wall Street is to watch people developing new forms of democratic decision-making. In the case of the Woolworth's strike, we don't know that much about what was going on inside the store. We know they developed their own committees to run things, and had an incredible culture of resistance, as historians would call it, but we also know that at the end, the big decisions about what they'd win were not, for the most part, under their control. So, we have to think about what we are modeling when we run occupations, in terms of what kind of a society, what types of relationships among ourselves we are building, and how gender and racial politics and class differences are going to play out.

You asked about the media. Much of the mainstream media was very supportive of the Woolworth strikers—that was a big part of what made it possible for them to stay in the store, and win. The headlines I used in the text are mostly real, although I made up the original title, "Girl Strikers Occupy Chain Store, Win Big." You would see headlines like that all the time during 1937. Today, you can see peeps here and there of sympathy—like one mainstream report on Occupy San Francisco that emphasized that the demonstrators had gone out of their way to isolate and discourage anyone who sought to damage a nearby ATM. The reporters and editors themselves are usually union members. But they're under tremendous pressure from their own bosses. So you almost never ever see a headline that affirms that Organizing Works! Striking Gets You Health Care! Warmongers Don't Invade Country X Because of Mass Protests!

Can you talk about this question of democracy within the occupation and the demands these young women, and we should say very young women, I think the average age was eighteen or nineteen, placed on the bosses? Within Occupy Wall Street there is a strong current of concern that raising any set of demands necessarily puts you at risk of being co-opted back into the system. So, how did Woolworth workers articulate their demands, and how, given this problem you raised about union officials taking over the negotiations, how do you see what we might call partial victories?

I have a tremendous respect for the process politics of Occupy Wall Street and the way that people have been experimenting with not moving too quickly toward saying, "Here's our one thing we want." They want to embrace so many issues, and that's really important. We absolutely need to think big about connecting the dots of social injustice. I myself think, though, that you have to have some concrete demands that you can win— and then you ask for lots more! That keeps you going, while you keep driving in your point about the big changes, and groping toward the middle-level road to those changes. You do need to feel a deep sense, however small, of "Gee, we did that. Look what we got," while simultaneously keeping clear that small steps will not solve the underlying problems. You have to have a sense as a movement that organizing worked, while being open to saying, "Wait a minute, did that lead us right back to where we were when we started?" André Gorz famously wrote in 1967 that you should ask for impossible demands that the system cannot satisfy.

In the case of the Woolworth strikers, they did win wage increases, improvements in working conditions, and union recognition, but they didn't solve the larger structural problem of Woolworth's as a huge capitalist firm following the logic of profit unfettered. They did put brakes on that exploitation, and they did help redistribute the wealth, if you take not just the Detroit case but all the organizing of retail clerks reaching well into the 1940s, inspired by the Woolworth's workers. But then you have to think about whether that movement then did or didn't contribute to a process of long-term structural change. Did it take on deep economic structures? Did it challenge capitalism, which continually regenerates wealth and inequality in its very nature?

One of the differences you raise between Woolworth's as it existed in the 1930s and Walmart today is the fact that, if Woolworth's began to incorporate international production into its supply chain in the 1930s, then Walmart today has taken the process to the most extreme degree possible. So, we see that most of Walmart's consumer goods come from China, from other Asian countries, all of which has to come through the ports, making Walmart a truly international corporation. And, in terms of the workforce, if Woolworth's refused to hire people of color in the 1930s, today Walmart employs black, white, Asian, Latino workers. They are young, middle-aged, elderly, men, women, gay, straight, and on and on. In other words, Walmart's workforce is tremendously diverse, despite the fact that Walmart's management retains discriminatory promotional and hiring policies. What are the specific challenges facing organizers in these circumstances?

Walmart is very specific because it is so global and so big, but the formula that it uses is the same used by Best Buy or Target or Starbucks or most any huge employer. They are looking for the cheapest labor they can get, they are driving labor costs down by making the job as simple as possible—exactly like Woolworth's did—and they'll take whatever cheap labor force they can find. Walmart is looking for whoever is most vulnerable and is going to have to take the job because they don't have other opportunities, in part because of racism and sexism. Of course, we know how badly Walmart has also been discriminating at higher levels of management. It also discriminates against older people, defining positions like clerks to include stocking shelves, so older people won't be able to do it, and the company saves on health costs. I think the sheer baldness of the way in which Walmart exploits all its workers gives people a common ground, because they know they are all getting the same bad wages, the same crummy benefits, if any. They all know they can be fired the minute their supervisor, who's watching them on a spy camera, doesn't like the way they just burped. It's an opportunity for unity.

There are all kinds of historical examples of working people successfully organizing together across racial and ethnic lines. In the Lawrence, Massachusetts, textile strike of 1912, for example, workers and organizers gave their speeches in literally dozens of different immigrant languages. In packinghouse workers' union campaigns in the 1910s, Polish, Irish, and African American workers figured out ways to strike together even though they had huge conflicts. Ethnic solidarity can aid a social movement when people draw on cultural resources in their communities to then build to broader solidarities. We know employers are always trying to drive a wedge between racial and ethnic groups. There's a long history of that. But there's just as long a history of people overcoming it.

One of the things that's changing today is that poor and working people are once again starting to realize that our problems are not about people failing individually. It's that all this company or this system has to offer me is poverty. During the Great Depression, even when everyone knew a third of the country was unemployed, a lot of people still thought at first it was their own individual failure somehow. They had to figure out it was the system that was failing *them*. Also, you have to believe that organizing works. Because you have to believe that if you take the risk of a sit-down strike or the risk of an occupation it's going to pay off. And that's where history matters. Because if you look at U.S. history, it's full of people going out on strike, full of people occupying things, saying, "¡Basta ya!, enough already!" People are always saying, "We are in this together and the only way out is together." But you have see that and you have to believe in that and you have to know it's possible.

That's why this Woolworth story is so beautiful. It's a true story, I didn't make it up! These were absolutely ordinary young women who had never done anything like that. Some of them were sixteen and seventeen years old. But they were also very careful about choosing the right moment because they knew that if they didn't choose the right moment they could fry. They had the media on their side, they knew how to frame their issues, how to present themselves. You have to be very careful about those things while believing deep in yourself that we can do this together.

You don't walk in there all by yourself and say, "Mr. Boss, would you pretty please give me a raise?" You go in there with three thousand people all at once, and you say, "This is wrong, the way you're treating all of us, and we are not going to accept it any more, and we have lots and lots of friends out there all lined up." You have to believe in that power and that's what solidarity is all about. But it's also about having a vision of a labor movement that's not just about one group of workers. It's about seeing the need to fight for broader social gains, including big demands on the state. Whether it's the antiracist movement, or immigrant rights, or gay rights, it's about seeing all of these movements as a larger fight for social justice. That's what's brilliant about Occupy Wall Street and the way they've framed this as the 1 percent against the 99 percent.

We see in the thirties that the old strategies of craft unionism and exclusion utterly fail to deal with the economic crisis and a series of new ideas and tactics replace them, like the sit-downs, occupations, and city-wide general strikes. It seems to me that today, although there are more progressive elements, labor is in a similar crisis. Less than eight percent of the working class has a union, manufacturing is globalized, millions of workers cross borders looking for work, the service sector is now huge, etc. All of this has presented the unions with a huge dilemma. It's true that some elements in the trade union leadership have welcomed Occupy Wall Street, but others have been hostile, or remained aloof, or are worried that it is too radical or too disconnected from the Democratic Party. So there is tension over these new questions, new methods, new tactics that Occupy Wall Street is developing and the traditional labor movement's practices. Given this, what is your opinion about the role the established trade unions can play and, perhaps, what they need to change?

There's a long history of debate within the labor movement over whether it should be narrowly defined for just a small group of workers who get some power through their own struggles, versus seeing the labor movement as something broad that includes all working people and their concerns and their social movements to address those concerns, whether it's immigration or gay rights or housing discrimination. The labor movement is most powerful when it understands itself as a social movement. And it's also strongest when it understands that rank-and-file workers, their neighborhoods, and their families are the driving force of social change, not just the union officials. In the thirties, ordinary people, the rank and file, were unleashed. Better, they unleashed themselves. So that's one big thing. The labor movement has to respect its own members and their creativity and power and their faith in themselves. This is tied in with racism and sexism at the top. We still have a problem of who top-level labor leaders are in many of our unions. People of color and women need to be in the top leadership, with power to define what the labor movement is and what its priorities are in terms of social justice on all fronts.

Historically, the labor movement has been incredibly diverse in terms of what people understand a workers' movement to look like. In fact, what most people today understand a labor movement to be—that what a union does is have a government-sponsored election and then bargain a contract and then, if a demand is not in the contract, it doesn't exist—that's not what the labor movement looked like for its first hundred and fifty years. Just as important, it hasn't always been the case that the labor movement and social movements address different forms of oppression. At its best, the labor movement has fused with and served other movements, like the women's movement or the Black freedom movement or Chicano power.

You were trained in a school of labor history exemplified by your mentor, David Montgomery, who just recently passed away, that started from the assumption that working-class people can run the world. A lot of people will agree that we need to protest because conditions are bad and we should try to fight for some reforms but there really is no alternative to capitalism. In other words, the idea the world can be fundamentally different, as they said during the French general strike in 1968, "The boss needs you, you don't need the boss," is a utopia. Do you believe that labor, working-class people of all colors and nations, men and women, can run the world? Or is that simply a dream that we should put aside in the interest of more practical politics?

Of course it's possible. You do, though, have to define working people as broadly as possible and that's why framing this as the 99 percent is really important. I think the ordinary people who go to work every day, they don't own big things, they don't have a lot of power in the formal sense, but they do know how to do their job, how to run that office, or hospital or school or factory or store or port, they know how to run it as well as the boss—and usually better. Famously, secretaries are always having to teach the boss how to do their job. And we have examples today like in Argentina, where people are successfully re-opening and managing their closed factories by themselves. There's a long history of co-ops and collectives and communes. You still have to duke it out and have a lot of arguments and a lot of meetings. Of course, you always have to have a lot of meetings! There are all sorts of other structures we know about, non-capitalist or pre-capitalist, in which societies are not based on the idea that one group of people owns things and exploits another group of people so that they can get even more money, right? Why should that be the organizing principle for how we manage our lives together? I think there is a tremendous wisdom and creativity and generosity among all people. Working people know that they could be doing it themselves, but we don't get to practice it very often. Our systems of governing ourselves don't have to be about these big, monolithic, global corporations paying off governments to change the rules so they have even more wealth. Then there's the challenge of how get there from here. Of course, it's a REALLY big challenge. How do we do it? We're not all going to just get along and agree with each other all the time; but that doesn't mean that we should then just agree to hand over all the wealth to the top 1 percent and say, "Thank you very much, yes, you can drive me into the ground." People aren't going to put up with that forever.

In the end, what the Woolworth strike shows is that regular people have this potential to change the world, and they often do. You have to believe that it's possible and you have to have the right moment and you have to do it together. But when people do move together—and in 1937 it wasn't just those Woolworth strikers, it was people all over Detroit, at General Motors, it was the union people, it was the money pouring in to the women from unions and individuals all over the country, it was about the people going out on strike in New York, all of it can come together. And it does come together all the time. It's happening all over the world as we speak. We have to organize to change the world. It takes a lot of small, daily organizing as well as a lot of frustration. But when the time is right and people feel historical change they want to be part of it. Then they do change the world—and change, themselves in the process.

Women Strikers Occupy Chain Store, Win Big

ON THE SURFACE it seemed like the most ordinary of Saturdays at the most ordinary of American institutions. It was February 27, 1937, at Woolworth's Five and Dime store, the big four-story red brick one in downtown Detroit, at the corner of Grand River and Woodward Avenue. Like all Woolworth's stores, this one was painted with red and green trim, with the chain's name out front in big gold letters. Throughout that morning cabs and buses, Chryslers and Plymouths slid back and forth along the avenue. Shoppers rustled by or paused for a brief chat with friends.

Inside, Woolworth's opened up like a palace, with fluted columns, embossed tin cciling tiles, hanging bulbous art nouveau lamps, and, best of all, a vast array of small, low-priced goods: hair combs, knitting needles, lampshades, safety pins, pie plates, face creams, and crisp new shoelaces folded into little packets with paper bands around their middles specifying their length. Most wonderfully, Woolworth's was a palace built for working-class people. The big fluted columns were made of concrete, not marble, then painted shiny bright colors. Tidily printed signs poked up from displays throughout the store to reassure customers that almost all the goods splayed out in flat, tray-like counters at waist level cost only five or ten cents, just as the store's name promised. Bins of tilted glass along one side held back masses of eminently affordable jelly beans, peanut clusters, and old-fashioned mystery candies with names of obscure origin like "bridge mix" or "nonpareils" (the little chocolate mounds with white sprinkles embedded in their tops that survive today in the equally obscure realm of movie theater candy).

Unlike its Costco and Price Club heirs, Woolworth's promised not a cavernous warehouse of cardboard boxes in monster sizes, but a maze of small nooks and crannies, up and down stairs, waiting to be discovered. Shoppers in downtown Detroit that Saturday could weave upward to the second floor on wide wooden stairs with a brass railing down their middle, pause on the landing at a glass display full of woven pastel Easter baskets and Peter Rabbits (it was three weeks before Easter) and pass upward to a "complete line of knitting and crotcheting" with "free instruction," and to the delights of the notions and dry goods departments. The more intrepid could follow arrows luring them down into the basement sales level, complete with canaries. There, shoppers who were white could indulge in a banana split at the lunch counter.

The hundred and fifty or so young women working at Woolworth's on this particular morning seemed like the most ordinary of young working-class ladies. Sandwiched behind the displays, gracefully sidestepping piles of boxes kept out of the customers' sight, the clerks flashed smiles, made change, or cheerfully introduced the latest lipstick. The ones who worked in the candy department and at the lunch counter wore little white short-sleeved uniforms with colored cuffs and collars and matching plastic buttons. The salesclerks, by contrast, were wearing surprisingly dressy outfits in somber colors—long, sleek, fitted skirts and knitted tops with short jackets or wide lace collars. Most wore heels, though not the waitresses, who had on the 1930s version of sensible shoes. Almost every single one of the women had the exact same hairdo: cut just a bit below her chin, parted on the side, and curving down in carefully constructed waves around her face.

Suddenly, at exactly 11:00 a.m., at the height of the Saturday shopping rush, Floyd Loew, an organizer for the Waiters' and Waitresses' Union of Detroit, strode to the very center of the store's first floor. Without warning he blew a screeching whistle as loud as he could and yelled, "STRIKE! STRIKE!" (Or by some reports, "STRIKE, girls, STRIKE!")

Voices shouted out and cheers rose from different parts of the store. First the women in the white uniforms at the food counter stopped working. Then they moved quickly through the whole store, and soon almost all the women workers on all three sales floors had stepped back from their counters or rushed out from the kitchen, folded their arms, and stopped working, clearly in accordance with a tightly coordinated plan.

"Behind the counters, the girls appeared ready for the call," reported the *Detroit News*. "The jangle of cash registers stopped, and bewildered customers found themselves holding out nickels and dimes in vain." A small number of women, maybe ten or fifteen, kept working for a while, and seem to have slipped quietly out of the store in the chaos that followed. One news report alleged that Floyd Loew, the union organizer, yelled out, "Sock any of those girls who don't stop working." But "there was no trouble," said the *Detroit Times*. "Not a girl tried to wait on a customer."

A floor supervisor rushed off to find the store's manager, William F. Mayer. Within minutes, Mayer and all the women, plus assorted stock boys, department heads, and managers, along with Loew and other organizers from the waiters' and waitresses' union, had crammed into a conference room on the third floor. The strikers presented Mayer with an explicit set of demands: they would refuse to work and would occupy the store night and day until Woolworth's granted them union recognition, a ten-cent-an-hour raise (they were making around twenty-five cents an hour), an eight-hour workday, time and a half for overtime after forty-eight hours a week, fifty-cent lunches for the soda fountain workers, free uniforms and free laundering of them, seniority rights, hiring of new workers only through the union offices, and no discrimination against the strikers after they returned to work.

Mayer hurriedly tried to "sweet-talk" the women into returning to work. He promised he'd do everything he could to address their concerns on Monday—if only they'd all, please, please, go back to work.

"Alright girls, give him your answer," shouted Loew. "NO!" they roared. And there was no turning back.

A hundred and eight ordinary young women had done a huge, astonishing thing: they were not only on strike, right in the depths of the Great Depression, but they were occupying the property of one of the largest transnational companies in the United States and refusing to leave until they won. It was a classic sit-down strike, but for the first time the strikers were all women working in a variety store, not men in a factory. Within hours the eyes of the nation would be riveted on these young women and their strike. They had, after all, taken on one of the biggest corporate and consumer icons of the century, with two thousand stores in five countries—it was like striking Walmart, the Gap, and McDonald's all at the same time.

These young women believed that they just might win because they were living in an extraordinary moment in history, in the exact geographic epicenter of the labor uprisings of the Great Depression. At that very moment union activists were breaking out of the straightjacket of the American Federation of Labor (AFL) to give birth to the militant Congress of Industrial Organizations (CIO). In a mass uprising of almost four million working people in the late 1930s and early 1940s, young people were on the move; the Left was thriving; new tactics of canny strategy and direct action, especially the sit-down strike, were suddenly deployed with both daring and shocking success. It wasn't exactly a revolution, but something huge was happening in early 1937.

And from February 27 to March 5, the Woolworth strikers were at center stage. Newsreel teams, radio personalities, and reporters from the *New York Times*, *Chicago Tribune*, and *Life* magazine rushed to Detroit to cover the story. As the press well knew, the salesclerks and waitresses at Woolworth's had set something huge in motion that would have ripple effects in the labor movement, in popular culture, and in the lives of everyone involved for decades to come. No question, these strikers had taken on Goliath. It was both thrilling and terrifying—and the consequences were utterly uncertain.

CHAIN STORE MENACE GROWING

Today, if we think of Woolworth's, we either recall the battles to desegregate its lunchrooms in the early 1960s or evoke a romantic image of small-town life gone by, paved under by the consolidating forces of modern consumer capitalism. But in the 1930s Woolworth's was itself the modernizer, bulldozing down an earlier generation of small merchants and offering shoppers not the old-fashioned but the new and stylish. In the process it spat out enormous profits for its owners. By the mid-1930s, though, the public was beginning to get clear about where those profits came from—and at what price.

Frank W. Woolworth, the firm's president until his death in 1919, opened his first store in Lancaster, Pennsylvania, in 1879. Woolworth figured out that he could draw in masses of working-class shoppers and make hefty profits by offering an entire store full of ultra-cheap goods, none of them priced at more than five or ten cents: hence the new name "five and dime." Within a few years Woolworth had opened seven stores in upstate New York and Pennsylvania; by 1905 he had a hundred and twenty stores all over the country; by 1937 he had over two thousand. Woolworth's immediately leapt across national borders. Between 1897 and 1900 alone the company opened fifty-nine stores in Canada. By 1913, Frank Woolworth had come of age as a famous magnate, big enough to erect his own monument, the Woolworth Building, a sixty-story neo-Gothic tower at the corner of Broadway and Park Place in New York City.

In part, Frank Woolworth's secret was all those inexpensive, useful objects—the safety pins, shoelaces, and pie plates. But he had also figured out that people would buy all sorts of other "novelty goods," another now old-fashioned concept that was innovative in its time. He sold millions of holiday decorations, for example, like the Easter bunnies on display in Detroit at the end of February in 1937, or glass ornaments for Christmas trees and funny green hats for St. Patrick's Day. His stores also catered to fads. Whatever hair clip happened to be in fashion that month, he stocked by the millions. And Woolworth also figured out there was money to be made off children, especially by selling candy; in 1917 alone the chain sold ninety million pounds. Woolworth's also established its famous segregated lunch counters, selling banana splits for pennies. Overall, even if the profit was miniscule on each nonpareil or chocolate sundae, the volume of total sales added up quickly. In 1935 Woolworth's produced a profit of $31,247,000.

Frank Woolworth also pioneered in the structural elements that could make economies of scale lucrative. He introduced a centralized, pooled ordering system, regional warehouses, and regular buying forays to Europe. In the process his company developed enormous power over its suppliers, as it began to skip past the wholesalers to buy directly from manufacturers—just as Walmart and its rivals do today. "The syndicate would absorb a factory's entire output under the terms of year-long contracts," notes James Brough in his study of the Woolworth family. "Frank dictated the terms to those manufacturers; the price of their security was subservience." With large markets assured, the suppliers could save by avoiding credit costs and buying raw materials in bulk. But Mr. Woolworth called the shots on price, quality, shipment dates, and future contracts.

Woolworth's goods were also cheap because Frank and his minions became adept at sniffing out the products of sweated labor. In one account of a buying trip, Woolworth told of visiting a poor mountain village in Germany where impoverished women and children labored night and day, heads bent, making little wax dolls and Christmas tree ornaments. Ah, Mr. Woolworth lamented, they were so oppressed. He immediately placed a big order.

At the time of the Detroit strike, the Woolworth Corporation was a powerful presence all over North America and across the Atlantic. That year Woolworth's owned 2010 stores in the United States, Canada, and Cuba, plus 737 stores in Britain and eighty-two in Germany.

But just as the company grew and grew, a broad social movement mushroomed with equal energy in the late 1920s and 1930s, dedicated to stopping the spread of chain stores like Woolworth's. By 1928, organizations dedicated to eradicating what they called the chain store evil were thriving in more than four hundred communities across the United States. Almost entirely lost to historical memory, the movement expanded throughout the early and mid-1930s and reached its peak at almost the exact same moment as the Detroit strike in 1937.

Critics pointed out that stores like Woolworth's had been marching across the national landscape at an ever-increasing pace since the 1920s. The chains' share of total retail sales grew from 4 percent in 1919 to 20 percent in 1929 and was still expanding. The A&P grocery chain alone owned fifteen thousand stores by 1929; chain groceries altogether accounted for more than 39 percent of all grocery sales in the country that year. Drugstores, cigar stores, shoe stores—in all these fields, chains were rapidly pushing aside locally owned businesses and independent merchants. In the variety store market Woolworth's dominated, well ahead of its closest rival, S. S. Kresge, with 1,881 stores in 1930 to Kresge's 678.

Small merchants in particular charged that the chains were "a menace to the community." As a letter circulated in Indiana put it, "The chain stores are undermining the foundation of our entire local happiness and prosperity. They have destroyed our home markets and merchants, paying a minimum to our local enterprises and charity, sapping the life-blood of prosperous communities"—sort of like corporate vampires. Small merchants couldn't compete with the chains' vast economies of scale, the critics charged, and as smaller stores went under, jobs for owners and their trainees were evaporating, leaving "a nation of clerks." Wholesalers were also being squeezed out by the growing intimacy between chain stores and suppliers, and they too jumped into the fray. By the mid-1930s the movement against chain stores had become extremely popular. A poll in August of 1936 found that 69 percent of Americans believed the chains were dangerous and should be suppressed.

In response, between 1934 and 1941 state legislators introduced five hundred bills containing measures designed to curb the chains. Most of the proposed laws imposed a hefty graduated tax that grew steeper as the number of stores in the chain grew, and most were quickly ruled unconstitutional, but thirty-two survived. In 1928, as criticism mounted, Congress ordered the Federal Trade Commission to investigate the chains. Its report, issued in 1935, came out pro-chain. But meanwhile, the mere fact that the federal government was investigating the chains confirmed popular concerns, further legitimating the anti-chain movement. The movement's greatest triumph was the Robinson-Patman Act of 1936, an amendment to the Clayton Antitrust Act of 1914. Robinson-Patman addressed the supply end, making it illegal for manufacturers to offer differential discounts to retail buyers based on the quantity of their orders, if the effect would be "to lessen competition or tend to create a monopoly."

By the mid-1930s the chains felt deeply threatened by all this agitation—the proposed taxes alone would have cost them millions. Woolworth's, as one of the largest and most visible of these retail empires, would have felt especially vulnerable. Very quickly the chains spent thousands on advertisements, lobbyists, and even a clever little *Debate Manual on the Chain Store Question* that purported to offer tips for arguing both sides but always circled back around to the dangers of regulation. By 1937, they had pushed back their critics and stopped the anti-chain movement's advance. Woolworth's public relations problem number one had been successfully contained for the time being, but its ghost would remain, hovering behind the strike to come.

BABS SPENDS MILLIONS ON NEW HUBBY IN ORGY OF SPENDING

The company's executives, though, could never contain their public relations problem number two, Woolworth heiress Barbara Hutton. Hutton proved an eternal public relations migraine because she unmasked one of the company's dirty secrets: how much money was being made and how offensively it was being spent. And when the Detroit sit-down blasted across the nation's headlines in 1937, Barbara Hutton loomed larger than ever in the public imagination.

Barbara was Frank Woolworth's granddaughter, born in 1912. Her mother, Edna Woolworth, had married eternal playboy Franklyn Hutton, brother to the famous broker E. F. Hutton. When Barbara, their only child, was four, Edna killed herself with poison. Barbara spent the next two years under the care of governesses, wandering about in her grandfather's mansion in New York. Then, in 1919, her grandfather passed on to wherever chain store magnates go, soon to be joined by his wife Jennie, and in 1924 the Woolworth fortune passed to their two surviving daughters plus little Barbara, in three equal shares.

That left Barbara "the richest girl in the world," as the press and its readers dubbed her, riveted by the prospect of her vast future wealth. For a time her father took an interest in her, but soon she was old enough to be packed off to boarding school in the East.

"Babs" became a fixture in the media throughout the 1920s, the proverbial pampered, unhappy, ultra-rich semi-orphan for whom the phrase "poor little rich girl" was originally coined.

Then the Depression hit, and Barbara came of age. Her self-indulgent persona blossomed, and everyone knew about it from daily press reports. She was infatuated with spending money —on jewels, on designer clothes, on cars, and especially on men. Out of some vast romantic fantasy and who knows what deep-seated insecurities she had developed during her famously unhappy childhood, Hutton was fixated on marrying European royalty. In 1933, five months before she turned twenty-one and could assume full control over her estate, she married Count Alexis Mdivani (with a nicely pretentious silent M), a Russian emigré gold digger with a dubious claim to a Georgian title. The press went wild. At the celebrity wedding of the decade, Barbara wore a diamond tiara, bracelet, and pearls, altogether worth a million dollars (about twelve million in 2000 dollars). She bought eighty outfits for her honeymoon, seventy trunks for the servants to cart them around in, and for her wedding night a nightgown that had been embroidered by two dozen cloistered nuns.

Later that year Barbara came into full possession of her fortune, an estimated eighty million dollars (about six hundred million in 2000 dollars). As the press obsessively recounted her wealth over the next three years, "Babs" kept up the show in escalating performances of spending, traveling all over the world and throwing money around with proverbial reckless abandon. By 1937 she had dumped her first prince and married another, Count Kurt Haugwitz-Reventlow, this one a minor member of the vestigial Danish landed nobility. That year—the year of the Detroit strike—she bought jewelry worth two million dollars, a Packard, a yellow convertible, two Rolls-Royces, a 157-foot yacht, and a mansion-estate in London. The latter cost about four to five million dollars and featured two ten-car garages, a boathouse, stables, tennis courts, two pools (one indoor, one outdoor), and, best of all, a bathroom made of ten thousand dollars' worth of marble, with sink and bathtub handles of gold, shelves of crystal, and heated towel racks. She employed thirty-one servants to keep it all neat and tidy.

All this wealth, self-indulgence, and obliviousness would be obscene in the best of times, but seven years into the Great Depression it was beyond appalling to most Americans. The Poor Little Rich Girl became the Most Hated Girl in America. "There has always been something fantastic and a little useless and stupid about Barbara Hutton," wrote columnist Adela Rogers St. John in 1937. Wherever Barbara went in the United States, cab drivers snubbed her and doormen slammed doors in her face. And wherever she went she carried the "Woolworth heiress" tag along with her. (Although she had sold a large hunk of her domestic Woolworth stock in 1930, she still owned part of the British subsidiary, and even if invested elsewhere, the money had all come from grandpa Woolworth.) Much to the chagrin of the Woolworth executives of her day, Barbara Hutton Mdivani Haugwitz-Reventlow's crime was not so much that she was rich, but that—unlike her aunts, for example, who were every bit as wealthy—she failed to follow all the unspoken rules of discretion by which the super-rich mask their wealth, enjoy it behind closed doors, and represent themselves to the public as tasteful and benevolent.

TIRED FEET, SAY FIVE AND DIME CLERKS

If Barbara Hutton focused public attention on Woolworth profits by showing exactly where they went, she also highlighted where they came from, because in the eyes of the press her antithesis was the poor, exploited young woman who labored as a Woolworth's clerk. In 1933 Bing Crosby released the hit song that would entwine the two in the public imagination for decades: "I Found a Million-Dollar Baby in a Five-and-Ten-Cent Store."

Woolworth's goods were so very cheap in part because the people that sold them were paid the lowest possible wages. Frank Woolworth put his formula bluntly: "We must have cheap help or we cannot sell cheap goods." More precisely, he couldn't make huge profits and keep expanding if he couldn't obtain inexpensive labor to keep his profit margin up.

To keep its labor costs in the basement, Woolworth's deliberately deskilled its sales operation—that is, it made its clerks' jobs as simple as possible. "The Woolworth chain takes the position that the salesgirls are primarily wrapping and change-making machines and they make little effort to pick for sales ability," observed one industry analyst in 1928. Woolworth's pioneered by placing its goods out on display, easily accessible to the customer, who no longer had to ask a clerk to fetch down a particularly enticing lampshade from an upper shelf behind a counter. The company bet correctly that if enough appealing objects were available at cheap enough prices, the goods would sell themselves and Woolworth's would save big bucks on labor. "When a clerk gets so good she can get better wages elsewhere, let her go," Frank Woolworth wrote as early as 1892, "for it does not require skilled and expensive salesladies to sell our goods."

Woolworth's formula is the same one used by McDonald's, Circuit City, and other big chains today. If the job is sufficiently deskilled, a huge potential labor pool opens up, and if turnover rates are high, so much the better—managers can then pick and choose the pliant, the eager, and the charming. By the 1930s, Woolworth's had developed labor policies that deliberately created a revolving door of employment. Store managers were rotated from store to store and encouraged to weed out employees regularly at each new site. And since the mid-nineteenth century employers had used another, accompanying trick: after deskilling the job, hire women—especially young women—who had very few choices on the labor market, who might see themselves working for pay only temporarily, and who, in theory, were less likely to unionize.

In 1937, Woolworth's employed about sixty-two thousand people in the United States, but never hired any African Americans. Or at least its managers didn't think they did. Throughout the mid-twentieth century, women of partial African descent passed as white, often by posing as Italian or Spanish, to obtain relatively good jobs as clerks in variety and department stores. However much these jobs were dead-end, poorly paid, and exhausting, they were a vast improvement over almost anything else available to Black women, leading hundreds of women who passed as white to endure the pain of hearing coworkers' racist remarks day after day in order to support their families.

Almost all the women who worked at Woolworth's in 1937 were very young. According to a national survey of Woolworth workers in 1930, about half the store's employees were sixteen, seventeen, or eighteen years old, a quarter were between nineteen and twenty-four, and only around 17 percent were twenty-five or older. Judging by photos of the Detroit strike, though, a very few of the Detroit workers were in their thirties or forties. Some, at the other end, were fourteen or fifteen. Former Detroit Woolworth's employee

Ceil McDougle, for example, remembers working at the chain in 1935 when she was only fifteen.

The women were overwhelmingly native-born, and most were of western or northern European descent, like McDougle, whose parents were English and Scottish. Some of the clerks and waitresses at Woolworth's were married, but most were single women who lived with their parents, turned their paychecks dutifully over to their elders, and got a few dollars slipped back now and again for a new dress or a pair of shoes.

Working at Woolworth's could be grueling. Although some worked only part-time or seasonally—Ceil McDougle worked only at Christmas, Easter, and other holidays—most worked around fifty hours every week, six days a week, and over a third regularly put in more than fifty-four hours. That meant nine hours a day, standing up. And that, in turn, meant very painful feet. "I don't know how the other girls stand it," sympathized a New York Woolworth's worker who had shelled out eight dollars for special shoes. "They get flat feet and fallen arches and little surface varicose veins." State labor laws might dictate a stool for every woman to rest on, but clerks at Woolworth's in New York laughed at the idea of getting to sit. "All the old girls know you can't sit down, no matter how slow it is and how tired you are." When business lagged, the salesclerks had to look busy or they'd be confronted by floor managers or fake shoppers lurking about to spy on them. If a waitress lacked customers, she was expected to scrub the shelves or those big concrete columns—that was why the paint looked so shiny and bright all the time.

Managers could be capricious or mean. As Ceil McDougle put it politely, with an understated sigh, "Well, they didn't have your interests at heart." Or, as a New York Woolworth's employee put it in 1939, "The manager's very grouchy. . . . If he says black is red, then black is red." Store managers tended to create a hierarchy of women's employment correlated with perceived beauty. The loveliest often got the better jobs as salesclerks, lunch counter waitresses were one notch down, and kitchen helpers ranked lowest on the ladder of perceived attractiveness and concomitant income and workload. The clerks got $14.50, the waitresses $13.50 a week (plus the latter had to pay for their uniforms and to have them laundered, although they received some additional income from tips). Lower-level managers, all male, also had their pets—workers who they thought were cute, from whom they might obtain a sexual favor, or who pleased them with a seemingly subservient manner.

All in all, by 1937 Woolworth's had built a powerful engine of wealth and poverty, a private empire that spread to Cuba and Germany, into small-town life, and into the daily lives of tens of thousands of young women. But by the late 1930s, the workings of that engine were also becoming increasingly visible to the American public. Woolworth's might be a great place to buy pie plates or Fourth of July bunting, but Barbara Hutton's exploits were sickening, the chains were being cast as an evil menace, and the woman behind the counter had a glazed, exhausted look in her eye—people saw it. Soon enough, all those public perceptions would turn out to be powerful weapons in the hands of the strikers.

AUTOWORKERS IN BIG VICTORY OVER GENERAL MOTORS; STAY-INS SPREADING

Woolworth's was a formidable opponent, but the women who clerked at the Detroit Woolworth's weren't stupid in taking on such an immense adversary. This was the 1930s, after all, and they were sniffing the activist wind. In the middle of the Great Depression, just when working people should have been feeling most vulnerable, most powerless, most at the mercy of corporations, the tide of labor activism rushed in and millions of ordinary working people suddenly believed in their own power and unleashed it.

The Great Depression had hit hard and stayed hard. By 1933, one-third of the country's workforce was unemployed and another third was underemployed, working part-time, or in marginal jobs. Production plummeted by two-thirds; bankruptcies rippled through cities, schools, banks, and small businesses, tearing apart families. President Franklin Delano Roosevelt, inaugurated in 1933, promised to close the economic abyss, but the first elements of his New Deal, while they provided direct aid for the poor, did not yet address structural changes in the economy.

The mere hint of federal support for the labor movement in the National Industrial Recovery Act of 1933, however, prompted a wave of strikes and organizing drives in 1933 and 1934. Cotton pickers in California, textile workers in the South, garment workers in New York, waterfront workers in San Francisco, teamsters in Minneapolis—all organized by the hundreds of thousands and launched mass strikes, proving that working people were eager to join unions and anything but passive in the face of economic devastation.

But they had one big problem on their hands: the American Federation of Labor (AFL). After a decade of governmental repression following World War I, most of the labor unions that had remained in the early 1930s AFL were narrow, largely interested in skilled workers only, and spectacularly suspicious and conservative in their attitude toward organizing new workers, especially women or people of color, whom they mostly excluded. Most AFL unions were obsessed with petty jurisdictional disputes over which union had the right to represent which exact workers, depending on narrow skill categories. (The federation's opponents called it the American Separation of Labor.)

Then, in 1935, Congress passed the National Labor Relations Act, also known as the Wagner Act, to deliberately encourage unionization and collective bargaining through a complex system of supervised elections, negotiations, and, above all, protection of the right to organize. The moment had come for labor to rise up. But unless something could be done to crack open the AFL, nothing would move, and progressive activists knew it.

Enter the CIO. In late 1935, leaders of several of the more militant unions in the AFL formed a new coalition, the Committee for Industrial Organization, the original CIO. They quickly drew up plans for a mass organizing drive that would embrace all workers in broad, industry-by-industry unions, and started to pool their funds. Deeply threatened by these militants and their energetic plans, the AFL leadership suspended all of the CIO's unions in late summer of 1936. Undaunted, the purgees formed their own new, independent federation, changed its name to the Congress of Industrial Organizations to keep their acronym the same, and the floodgates of organization finally opened up.

All through the fall of 1936—the fall before the Woolworth's strike—CIO organizers fanned out into industrial communities in the northeastern and midwestern United States. The United Mine Workers (UMW) alone, led by the famous John L. Lewis, donated half a million dollars to build the Steel Workers' Organizing Committee (SWOC). Within a few months, more than a hundred thousand steelworkers in a hundred and fifty different towns had rushed to join. Meanwhile, CIO organizers wove together a welter of small auto workers' unions into a new, unified body, the United Auto Workers (UAW). Throughout that fall, UAW members led small, sporadic strikes at parts plants and other factories in the upper Midwest, nothing huge, but December brought the first sign of what was about to come: UAW workers who made brakes at the Kelsey-Hayes plant in Detroit won a sit-down strike.

Then, suddenly and unexpectedly, the UAW took on General Motors, the largest corporation in the world. On December 30, 1936, in Flint, Michigan— about seventy miles outside Detroit—auto workers staged a sit-down strike at the General Motors Fisher Body plant. The Flint strike, in turn, forced the company to stop production at other plants all over the country, idling 112,000 workers. Riveted, the nation watched for six weeks as the strikers camped out in the plant, the National Guard camped in the streets, the governor refused to send soldiers into the buildings, and local police and strikers battled it out with tear gas both inside and outside the plant. Finally, miraculously, on February 11, 1937, the mighty General Motors capitulated to the pipsqueak United Auto Workers and agreed to recognize the union and to negotiate wage increases and better working conditions. The nation was stunned. The greatest of corporations had been brought to its knees. Suddenly anything was possible.

For a few days local people absorbed the news. Then all hell broke loose in Detroit. In the second week after the General Motors settlement, four or five thousand working people at twenty or thirty different workplaces throughout the city went on strike. Some just walked out the old-fashioned way; others sat down. On Monday, February 22, for example, three hundred auto body workers at Briggs Manufacturing in Highland Park stopped work and occupied their plant. On Tuesday, thirty men who drove liquor trucks for the Star Transfer Lines struck and won their demands in a single day. On Wednesday, three hundred women and a handful of men who worked at the Ferry-Morse Seed company staged their own sitdown strike, and at the Conant Factory Lunch, sixty high-school boys who delivered food to local factories sat down and after five hours won a pay raise from $1.00 to $1.25 an hour. That very night fifty-five charwomen who cleaned the Penobscot Building won a raise in pay after a two-hour work stoppage of their own.

The strikes and victories went on and on. On Thursday the Ferry-Morse Seed workers won their strike with a ten- to twenty-five-cent an hour pay increase and a forty-hour work week. At the Bon Dee Golf Ball Company, six workers sat down; workers at the Splendid Laundry announced they'd won a pay increase. At the Massachusetts Laundry, "300 girls sat down and demanded a straight ten cents an hour increase." Organizing worked.

Every day the women who worked at the downtown Detroit Woolworth's would have read about these events in the paper and heard about them on their radios. Every day they would have heard tales of daring actions from neighbors and friends, sisters and brothers, boyfriends, fathers, and mothers. Every day they would have had more time to think about the General Motors victory and all the subsequent gains workers in Detroit were winning with their strikes. And every day they would have wondered if they could do it too.

On Saturday morning they all showed up at work, in their tidily pressed uniforms and sleek dark skirts. They'd heard enough to make up their minds.

MANAGEMENT TO WOOLWORTH STRIKERS: DROP DEAD

Saturday, February 27, 11:30 a.m. Upstairs, in that all-important meeting, manager Frank Mayer had tried his sweet talk, but to no avail; the women had shouted back "no." Now they were out on strike for real—they'd done it. But what came next?

First, and most urgently, they needed to secure the doors to make sure none of their fellow workers defected. Mayer had already rushed his own guards to the doors to keep new customers out.

Quickly the strikers and their allies from the waiters' union took over the doors from management and seized store keys from other employees—stock

boys, waffling salesclerks—who remained. Within minutes "a huge crowd
… gathered at the Woodward Avenue doors," reported the *Detroit Times*, "but
nobody was admitted. Vigilant girl strikers guarded all doors."

That still left around two hundred "amazed" customers trapped inside the
store. A few fled out the door immediately, but it soon became clear that
most of them wanted to stay and watch the excitement. "The management
sought to get the public out, but the customers wanted to remain and view
a sit-down strike first hand," said the *Detroit News*. Woolworth's shoppers,
after all, were themselves working-class men and women, conscious of the
city's sit-down strikes of the previous weeks and perhaps quite sympathetic.
Some of them might even have known the strike was about to happen and
been in the store deliberately. Gradually, over the next hour, Mayer and the
other managers hustled them out, a handful at a time.

Inside, it wasn't clear what would happen next. Curious faces started to press
against the glass out front, so Mira Komaroff, from the waiters' and waitresses'
union, organized a group of women to lower all the blinds and cover the street-
level windows with brown wrapping paper from the store. Then they rolled
out sheets of the same paper over the counters, covering the merchandise as
the clerks always did at the end of the day.

From the very beginning, the occupiers started to enjoy themselves
immensely—and that would prove a key to their power and solidarity during
the strike. According to the *Detroit Free Press*, as the women left Mayer's office,
they "laughed and shouted and paraded up and down the stairways in a noisy
celebration." They mobbed the three pay phones at the back of the main floor
to call their relatives and warn them excitedly that they might be in the store
indefinitely, joking, "You better expect me when you see me." One large group
settled down in little clusters on the stairs; others huddled at the counters
and started playing checkers. Someone pulled out a deck of cards decorated
with polka dots and a pair of little Scottie dogs on the back and started a game
with three other women at the lunch counter.

But what, exactly, was going on? Would they be in the store for seven
weeks, like the General Motors strikers in Flint? Or had they just signed up
for a three-hour tour, like most of the Detroit workers who had staged
quickie sit-downs the week before?

By noon the store was caught in a strangely suspended state: it was filled with
food, all set up for the lunch rush. But the strikers carefully "kept away from
the counters where food was spread out ready for the luncheon crowd." Instead,
some of the women who'd brought bag lunches began to share them around,
offering sandwiches and celery sticks, laughingly peeling bananas and feeding
them to each other. At 1:30, Frank Mayer appeared at the top of the stairs and
boomed, "Go downstairs and have lunch. It's on the house." The strikers cheered

him and crowded to the counters, "where the piles of fruit and rows of pies disappeared quickly, adding to the good natured tone of the strike." Meanwhile the guards persuaded the last few customers to slip out the door.

All that food produced a rush of good feeling toward Frank Mayer. "To show their gratitude, they washed the dishes afterward," the *Detroit Free Press* reported. At this point Vita Terrall, the women's leader throughout the strike and the only individual striker the papers identified fully, began to speak directly to reporters. She was married, twenty-four years old, and worked at the candy counter. Terrall told the press after lunch that "they all like[d] Mayer and had 'nothing against him'"; the real battle, she said, was against the regional Woolworth's management in Cleveland. Floyd Loew, the organizer, had made the same argument to the strikers during lunch: "Your quarrel is not with the resident manager. . . . Stick by him. The quarrel is with the company." ("Loew's speech brought cheers between bites.")

Then suddenly the other shoe fell, and it all got very serious. Mayer was only the local store manager, and at 2:00 his boss, A.J. Dahlquist, the district superintendent for Woolworth's forty stores in the Detroit area, showed up. Vita Terrall rounded everyone up onto the main stairwell between the first and second floors, the only place large enough for all to fit, for another meeting. Louis Koenig, business agent for the waiters' and waitresses' union, once again presented the strikers' official demands, this time to Dahlquist: a ten-cent an hour raise, union recognition, time and a half for overtime after forty-eight hours, no charge for uniforms or for their laundering, seniority rights within each department, free lunches for the soda fountain workers up to fifty cents a day, and all new employees to be hired through the union office. It was quite a list—note how the demands included monetary issues but also shorter hours of work and, very importantly, regulation of the employment process: a codified system of seniority to counter the capricious and often sexually insidious decisions of individual managers, and a regularized system of initial employment in which Woolworth's management could hire only union members.

In reponse, Dahlquist told Koenig, the strikers, and their allies essentially to drop dead. He had spoken to the Woolworth's district manager, O. L. Gause, he said, on the phone in Cleveland, and had an ultimatum: "There will be no negotiation under any circumstances until the union organizers have left and the store is emptied. . . . The store must be turned back to us." Then he upped the ante: if the strikers didn't leave immediately, Woolworth's would lock out the workers at all its other thirty-nine stores in Detroit. "We will close every store in the city if necessary for an indefinite period."

Most amazingly, the strikers were completely undaunted. They greeted Dahlquist's ferocious and quite serious ultimatum "with some giggling, a modicum of jeering and great derisive shouting," according to the *Detroit News*. Vita Terrall then stepped forward. "If we leave here we are licked," she told the women. "We simply must remain in the store."

"Are you going to stick?" she asked.

"We'll stick!" they shouted back. "We'll stay until the cows come hom," a few piped in. And once again the women erupted in the choruses of voice and song that would carry them through their whole strike. First they belted out "America" over and over again, in Dahlquist's face. Then they sang other "patriotic songs."

By this time word had spread across the city of what the Woolworth's strikers had done, and visitors from the Detroit labor movement began to join them on the stairs to express solidarity. (Dahlquist must eventually have slunk away.) Bill Marshall, president of UAW Local 7 at the Chrysler plant, showed up. So did Frances Comfort from the Detroit Federation of Teachers. "I was really thrilled when I heard what you cute kids had done," she told the strikers. "Some people say you're lawbreakers, but I'm here, a school-teacher, proud to be among you. Many of you girls were in my classes in school and there you were trained to expect something from life." But here they were instead, she said, "working for a hopeless pay.... You are fighting not only for yourselves, but for thousands of girls like yourselves all over the country." It was all a spectacular ritual of solidarity, and enormous fun.

But Dahlquist's ultimatum had been a serious one. And it was now clear that this wasn't just a three-hour tour. Dahlquist agreed to meet on Sunday at 2:00 p.m. with Louis Koenig of the Waiters' and Waitresses' Union, plus representatives of the cooks' and retail clerks' unions—each of whom, in classic AFL fractional style, claimed jurisdiction over a different group of Woolworth's workers. That meant, at the very least, that the women would be in the store for the night and well into the next day. "Now the women's work was cut out for them," as Floyd Loew later put it.

FIVE AND DIME STRIKERS SETTLE IN FOR LONG STAY; UNION OFFICIALS RUSH IN

By the time the Woolworth's women had launched their strike, though, workers in the Detroit area, across the United States, and throughout Europe had fine-tuned the art of the sit-down strike. In a strike of any sort, the workers have a basic goal: to shut down the employer's business by withholding their labor. To do so, they need to keep their own ranks solid so that none of the workers returns to work, and they also need to prevent strikebreakers from getting in to do the job. In conventional strikes of the 1930s, workers tried to mount thick, raucous picket lines outside the workplace, both to keep scabs from entering and to shore up their own spirits. There was always the very concrete risk that employers would send in police, private security, or belligerent scabs to force their way through the picket line and reopen the workplace. A sit-down strike offered multiple advantages over a conventional strike. First of all, scabs (managers today like to clean up their reputation by referring to them as "replacement workers") couldn't take over the jobs of the striking workers because the strikers were still right there, in the workplace. Moreover, employers would be less inclined to send in the police to force out the strikers because they'd then risk damaging their own property—that was part of the cleverness of a sit-down. And if they did drag people out of the workplace, they'd have to do so violently, producing unsavory publicity for the company. The strikers, meanwhile, didn't have to survive icy temperatures on the picket line (it dropped to twenty-six degrees in Detroit on February 27)—they were cozily ensconced inside, and if management decided to turn off the heat, well, that might mean more bad publicity, frozen pipes, or even dangerous fires. Labor activists had also discovered that sit-down strikes raised the morale of the strikers. Squished in together, rather than isolated at home or in small conversations on the picket line, the strikers enjoyed themselves and an enormous group feeling developed—precisely the sense of solidarity that working-class struggle is all about.

No one really knows when or where sit-down strikes were first invented. Frank Murphy, the pro-labor governor of Michigan at the time of the Woolworth's strike, claimed that masons for the pharaohs of Egypt used sit-downs to address grievances in the tomb-building industry. In 1715, workers hired to build the Rouen Cathedral in Lille, France, staged a sit-down strike. English textile workers tried it in 1817. Closer to home, in 1884, workers at the Jackson Brewery in Cincinnati barricaded themselves behind beer barrels for sixty-five hours. The Industrial Workers of the World (IWW) experimented with a sit-down strike in Schenectady, New York, in 1906.

Only in the mid-1930s, though, did the sit-down emerge as a popular and tremendously effective weapon for working people. In 1934, 1935, and 1936, miners in Yugoslavia, Hungary, Poland, Spain, Greece, Wales, England, and France all sat down. In May and June of 1936, almost one-fifth of all wage-earners in French factories and stores staged sit-down strikes. Well aware of what their brothers and sisters were up to in Europe, U.S. unions soon began to experiment with the strategy of occupying workplaces, especially meat-packing and auto plants, where activists began to perfect the "quickie" sit-down, by which a short strike for modest demands could produce results in a matter of hours. In 1936 a total of 34,565 U.S. workers occupied their workplaces in seventy different strikes; most were less than a day long. All this meant a wealth of collective experience. By the end of February 1937, the

Detroit labor movement in particular had refined its support systems, especially regarding the key logistics of food, bedding, and publicity.

In this explosive context, the Woolworth's workers were experimenting with their own use of a sit-down strike, and feeling out how organized labor might aid them. According to one account, several of the strikers had been members of Local 705 of the Waiters' and Waitresses' Union of Detroit before the strike; but another account of equal reliability reported that none had previously been union members. Whichever was the case, it's clear that the women initiated their actions entirely on their own, led, we can speculate, by their own Vita Terrall.

The women didn't, it turns out, just suddenly jump into action when Floyd Loew blew the whistle. The details are sketchy, but at some point on Friday morning—that is, the day before—a group of women had met with manager Frank Mayer and presented their demands. He reportedly "promised to comply with their demands as far as he could." Not satisfied, the women held a big meeting that Friday night, at which they formed themselves into a union. Again on Saturday morning they presented their demands to Mayer. Again he waffled, with a few promises of minor raises. It was then that they decided to sit down—even though, we can note, they'd already won a bit by simply organizing a union and presenting demands.

After the strike had commenced, Mayer whined duplicitously, "[It] came without warning. No one presented any demands to me formally." He conceded that "some of the girls spoke to me about laundry bills yesterday, and the store has agreed to shoulder this responsibility." He also claimed to have raised the waitresses' pay by a dollar a day, and announced magnanimously that new "girls starting to work today" would be "hired at 29 cents an hour rather than 28 cents." Of course that wouldn't help the strikers one whit; nor had Mayer put any of his offers in writing. "Sure we got a raise," wisecracked one striker. "What are we going to do with that—buy gum?"

At some time during the day on Friday, representatives of the Woolworth's workers had also paid a visit to the waiters' and waitresses' union (Local 705 of the Hotel Employees and Restaurant Employees' International Union, or HERE), in the nearby Lawyers' Building. "The Woolworth girls came to our offices with a list of demands and asked us to help get them," Mira Komaroff recalled. From that point onward and to the very end, staff members and rank-and-filers from Local 705 would play crucial roles in the Woolworth's strike.

Local 705 had three very distinct characters on its staff that day. The first, and oldest, was Louis Koenig, the secretary-treasurer of the local and very much the man in charge. Koenig (he pronounced it Kerr-nik), about forty-nine at the time, was a taciturn fellow who almost never smiled, hence his nickname "Smiley." Koenig had been born in Rohatyn, Austria, and had come to the United States when he was fifteen. He'd worked for a while as a waiter at the New York Stock Exchange Club and then become an officer of the Hotel Employees and Restaurant Employees' Union in New York. In 1916 Koenig moved to Detroit, where he and his pals working at the Detroit Athletic Club, almost all immigrant men from Europe, formed Local 705, the waiters' union. After four years as the local's president, Koenig moved into its leading staff position and was still there in 1937.

Koenig was a typical old-guard AFL business unionist. His local—and it was very much *his* local—represented around six hundred people in the mid-1930s, most of them waiters at the big downtown hotels and a few elite clubs. During the Prohibition era, Koenig had obtained most of the union's contracts by picketing, or threatening to picket, illegal bars and restaurants that served booze. If the cops showed up, the joints would be busted, so it was easier for employers to just sign with the union. Koenig's methods brought a few members into the local, but only from the top down. Rank-and-file members had little role or presence in the local, and he wanted it that way. Perhaps a dozen of its members were African American. They weren't allowed into the union's meetings at all. Known as the "Paradise Valley group," they had to meet separately in the basement.

Louis Koenig was never happy about allowing women into his union, either. In 1925, Local 705 had merged with a new Detroit waitresses' union, but twelve years later Koenig remained hostile to organizing women. "They get married and have babies," he was still complaining in 1972. "It's a devil of a job keeping up with them." Koenig's attitude was classic. In the mid-1930s almost all the AFL unions were hostile to allowing women into the labor movement. Stereotypes abounded: women were flighty, only interested in marrying, only in the labor force temporarily; white-collar workers like secretaries and store clerks weren't real "workers" worthy of the labor movement. Some AFL unions, such as the building trades, machinists, and coal miners, actively kept women workers out of their unions and froze them out of employment in their fields altogether. Nonetheless, women workers constituted around 10 percent of all AFL members at the time. The vast majority of them were in the big garment workers' unions, in textile unions, or in scattered unions representing waitresses, laundry workers, and agricultural workers.

Would the rising CIO change all that? In February of 1937 it didn't necessarily look that way. After all, the big thrust of CIO organizing in the fall of 1936 had been in mass production: steel, autos, rubber, and electrical manufacturing. Except for the latter, workers in these fields were overwhelmingly male; so were the hundreds of activists who had gone out to organize them. Because the CIO explicitly committed itself to the whole-industry organizing principle rather than craft-by-craft jurisdictions, in theory it would embrace all unskilled workers and therefore would help organize women. But in practice almost all its energy so far had gone into organizing men. When the UAW had so spectacularly organized General Motors in the Flint sit-down strike that winter, it had banned GM's female clerical workers from joining the union.

For all his hostility to women unionists, Louis Koenig saw the handwriting on the restaurant walls. In 1933, he met a politically passionate young woman, Mira Komaroff, and offered her a job on his union's staff. At first he only let her work as a secretary, but soon she was off organizing female hotel and restaurant workers as well as men, and eventually Koenig was referring to Komaroff as his protegée.

By all accounts, Mira Komaroff had a spectacular personality: she was energetic, sharp as a tack, and could charm just about anybody—the kind of woman that writers of the time described as "vivacious" and a "firebrand." Thirty years after her death, people who knew her, whatever they thought of her politics, still get an admiring grin on their faces at the mention of her name; she had a rare, special charisma. In photographs she smiles right into the camera and decades later looks as though she could walk right out of the picture and talk you into anything.

Mira Komaroff was twenty-three in February of 1937. She came from a middle-class Detroit family; her dad sold insurance and real estate. She'd attended Carnegie Tech in Pittsburgh for a year, studying interior design, but had to drop out as the family's finances shriveled with the Great Depression. So she came back to Detroit and jumped into labor and left-wing politics. In the middle years of the Depression—1933 to 1935—Mira belonged to the Proletarian Party, a Marxist group that had split off from the Socialist Party in 1919. The Proletarian Party was famous for its educational activities—soapbox speakers, public meetings, and monthly study groups for its members, which Mira attended regularly. Through the party Mira deepened her understanding of class relationships in the United States and of the need for working-class self-organization. She quickly became a key figure in Louis Koenig's Local 705, working to expand the union in downtown Detroit hotels and restaurants.

Then Floyd Loew showed up, and Mira was not happy about it. Loew was older—about thirty-five in 1937—a "tough, muscular" guy who allegedly "could talk as effectively as he could use his fists." (One union dissident later alleged that Loew had pushed him down a flight of stairs at the local's office.) Loew had grown up as a poor Michigan farm boy and then worked his way around the country as a waiter, becoming active in Hotel and Restaurant locals in Los Angeles and Miami. He came to Detroit in 1935, where he got a job waiting tables on the breakfast shift at the Book-Cadillac Hotel, and he too got involved with the Proletarian Party. In early 1936, Koenig hired Loew as an organizer. By all accounts, he was a great organizer—aggressive, energetic, and persuasive (but not "vivacious"—men never got to be "vivacious"). Mira Komaroff was deeply threatened by Floyd Loew. He was on her turf, he was outshining her, he was older, and he was a man. In late 1936 Koenig gave him a big raise; now he made more money than she did. Komaroff, meanwhile, had been offered a job by Governor Frank Murphy, with the Michigan Employment Security Commission; by early 1937 she was working full-time at the commission and only organizing for Local 705 at night and on the weekends.

Throughout January and early February, Loew, Komaroff, and Max Gazan, of the local cooks' union, had all worked together supporting the Flint General Motors sit-down strike. Once again the gender politics had gotten a bit thick. In the first days of the massive strike, auto workers' wives had set up soup kitchens to feed the hundreds of strikers inside the plant. They were overwhelmed with work, so the UAW called on the cooks' and waiters' unions for help. "We'll take care of it," Loew offered. "But tell the women to pick up their damn pots and pans and clear the hell out of here." This does not suggest that Loew would have been entirely respectful of the female strikers at Woolworth's—or of Komaroff.

Certainly, though, Koenig, Komaroff, and Loew each brought crucial assets to the Woolworth's workers. For one thing, their organization legitimated the strike. The strikers were now supported by an established union, with officers and everything, part of the larger Hotel Employees and Restaurant Employees' International Union, a national body. (By AFL jurisdictional etiquette, however, the clerks would be assigned to the retail clerks' union if the strike succeeded, even though that union played only a token role in helping them.) All three staffers from the waiters' and waitresses' union had highly developed negotiating skills, and they quickly took over that end of the strike—it was Koenig, not Vita Terrall, who presented the women's demands to Dahlquist on the stairwell; it was Koenig, plus male officials from the cooks' and retail clerks' unions, who arranged to meet with the managers on Sunday. Finally, both Komaroff and Loew had experience with the complex logistical details of figuring out how over a hundred people could eat, drink, and sleep over in a five-and-dime store with only a few hours' notice. That didn't necessarily mean they entirely knew what they were doing. "It was a real grass root [sic] movement and we were really green and ... almost got run over," Loew recalled fifty years later. "We were all new and without experience."

For the most part we can only speculate about the concrete interactions and negotiations between the strikers and the organizers. We do know that before they broke up their raucous meeting on the stairwell that Saturday afternoon, the Woolworth's strikers began to organize themselves internally, with help, evidently, from Loew and Komaroff. They elected Vita Terrall as Strike Committee Chair and then formed themselves into seven other committees: Food, Store Clean-up, Sales, Health, Cheer-Up, Entertainment, and Scrapbook.

Immediately the women sent word out to their families and friends that they needed mattresses and blankets. In mid-afternoon, Koenig and Charles Paulsen, from the cook's union, arrived with a truckload of mattresses, and the remaining strikers who hadn't volunteered for any committee now formed a Bed Committee to carry them. The mattresses were the old kind, of blue-and green jacquard fabric with big white floral designs and thick stitched borders. Tugging and pulling, the strikers splayed them out along the first-floor aisles, sideways, just barely fitting, so the women's heads and toes were almost up against the counters. They'd have to sleep three to a mattress; each got her own brightly colored plaid or striped blanket.

The women spent the rest of the afternoon perfecting the whole layout and, once again, partying hard. "Radios blared . . . and the clerks and fountain girls celebrated their own daring by dancing in the aisles." Various friends passed cigarettes into the store, and the women set up a smoking section in the basement, which had a tiled floor. They mobbed the phones once again, and again took up cards, checkers, and singing—all the while posing for photographs, sometimes exuberantly, sometimes coyly, and sometimes with a look of giggling astonishment at what they had done.

Dinner was once again on the house, Mayer offered, so they ate up the ice cream, hot dogs, and piles of jelly donuts arrayed on polished metal pedestals atop the counters. Mira announced that 11:00 p.m. would be curfew time. Slowly the chaos settled down. All the men in the store left, except for Floyd Loew, the union organizer, and Frank Mayer, the store manager, who dragged cots upstairs. Mira stayed too, downstairs. The women gradually giggled and whispered themselves to sleep. These were very young women, many of whom had never spent the night away from home before, and they were, after all, lying in the dark on the cold wooden floor of a four-story variety store.

Suddenly someone let out a scream, and then more screams spread across the store. A rat had jumped onto one of the mattresses, and in its own panic at the first screech began leaping across mattress after mattress, trying to escape. Panic broke out. Many of the women were ready to leave right then and there. But a quick huddle among Floyd, Mira, Vita, and a few others produced a solution: the women dragged their mattresses up to the second floor, where, in theory, rats would fear to tread, since there was no food on that level. Finally they all settled down—rats, strikers, organizers, and the boss—and the first day of the Woolworth's strike was over.

CANARIES JOIN SONG RAISED BY WOOLWORTH GIRLS
AS PRIMPING REPLACES CLERKING

Sunday, February 28. Curfew lifted at 8 a.m. The strikers crawled out of bed, got out their compacts, put on their makeup, and prepared for the reporters who, they knew, were about to rush in. "We had plenty of mattresses, blankets, and pillows and all of us slept well," Vita Terrall told the press.

Saturday had been dramatic, to say the least, and lots of fun amidst all the confrontation, but now the women settled into a daily routine. Now the committee structure kicked in. Now their friends came by and slipped them nightgowns, toothpaste, more blankets, cosmetic cases, and more cigarettes, which the women piled up on the counters in the basement. Floyd and Mira warned the strikers not to touch a thing that belonged to the store, but they seemed to have touched quite a lot, even if the counters were carefully covered with the brown wrapping paper. All those useful objects for which Woolworth's was so famous became, well, useful; the novelty items, lots of fun. The Sales Committee carefully kept track of it all: the strikers didn't steal or hurt anything, they just did a little shopping.

The Health Committee had a bit of work to do, too. Within the first twenty-four hours there was a run on "headache tablets." Reporters also noted, somewhat intrusively, that the change in the women's diet caused constipation, so someone brought in a supply of mineral oil and the women were all required to swallow a big spoonful every morning, under the supervision of a physician who showed up every day. The women joined in daily sit-ups and other calisthenics, too.

They also tightened up the food logistics. On Sunday morning, the strikers kicked out the manager for good, and took over the food operations themselves. From now on volunteers from the cook's union, coordinated by Floyd Loew, prepared their food in a kitchen set up outside, then carried it in to the lunch counter in the basement, where the women served each other. The strikers, after all, included waitresses, bakery assistants, and cooks. Some of the food they prepared themselves in the store's own kitchen. It was all brilliantly convenient. At Woolworth's—in contrast to those famous strikes in automobile factories—the women had a kitchen, cleaning supplies, headache tablets, safety pins, plus bathrooms and a candy counter all right there.

They set up systems for daily maintenance too: the Clean-up Committee swept floors, washed counters, and watched for rats. One group of women took care of feeding the canaries and cleaning their cages in the basement. As time passed, some of the strikers started washing clothes in the store's various sinks and hung them out to dry on the fire escape. In other words, they made themselves at home.

All this time they stayed in close contact with their friends and families, sweethearts, and husbands through constant phone calls on the store's three phones and furtive contacts through the front door. The situation was clearly stressful for some or the women wouldn't have formed their Cheer-Up Committee. "This committee served as a very important committee," Floyd Loew later wrote, "because most of the young women still lived at home and this endeavor was an overwhelming experience for such young participants." In another memoir, he recalled, "The Cheer-Up Committee was made up of a smiling and bubbly bunch of women and they were really needed. They watched for the first curling lip and they soon had all sadness chased away."

All in all, though, the strikers were still having a great time. A Pathé Newsreels team that showed up Sunday commented with a bit of puzzlement, "They seem to enjoy themselves despite the troubled atmosphere." These young women were used to working six days a week, nine hours a day, standing on their feet the entire time. All of a sudden they not only had the day off, but they could play all they wanted. By that morning they had changed into sensible shoes, T-shirts, and pants.

Some of the women played with the canaries; some of them gathered in small groups and played cards and checkers. Two women in loud plaid playsuits with matching square caps slid down the banisters, over and over. Dozens sat on the main stairwell and took up knitting, crocheting, and embroidery, utilizing the second floor's cornucopia of embroidery hoops, knitting needles, and skeins of yarn.

The women moved in on the sheet music department, too, and sang on the stairs for hours and hours. (A newsreel captures them swaying back and forth on the stairs, singing, one playing a mandolin, another holding, mysteriously, a toilet plunger.) A favorite, which they sang over and over again, was "Hail, Hail, the Gang's All Here." They also liked "Pennies from Heaven" and rewrote a verse of "John Brown's Body" as "We'll Hang Old Woolworth to a Sour Apple Tree." Another favorite was "Mademoiselle from Armentieres," to which they made up their own words:

Sit down girls, sit down girls, parlez-vous.
Sit down girls, come sit down, don't be afraid to [stand your ground?].
Hinky dinky parlez-vous.

Someone hauled in a Victrola; records appeared. Radios blared. They danced in couples. The Entertainment Committee organized "impromptu entertainments" (what they were exactly, we'll just have to leave up to our imaginations). And they arranged for the musicians' union to show up nightly for free concerts, to which they also danced.

We know much of this because much of it took place in front of dozens of reporters—not just those faces pressed to the glass out front, but *Life* maga-zine, famous national radio broadcaster H. V. Kaltenborn, the *Chicago Tribune*, the *New York Times*, the *Daily Worker*, *Women's Wear Daily*, Pathé Newsreels, and three dailies and one weekly newspaper from Detroit, among others. The media world rushed in, but what did it see? Kaltenborn, the radio man, loved the strike: "The CIO unions might want to take lessons from the Five-and-Ten cent crew on strike strategy," he told the nation. For Kaltenborn, the strike was a serious demonstration of how to build a powerful labor movement.

But for almost all the other reporters the occupation was anything but serious. Rather it offered an opportunity to trivialize the women as silly girls playing strike and to titillate readers with their alleged obsession with beauty and boys. Every single report described the strikers as "girls," never as women, although most were over the age of eighteen, and many were in their twenties, thirties, or forties. Their gender was always identified; they were always "girl strikers," unlike the General Motors sit-downers, for exam-ple, who were "striking workers," and almost never "boys" except very rarely in a jovial, comradely sense. Even the Communist Party's *Daily Worker* couldn't resist referring to the women's hair color and body type: "Young girls, blonde, brunette, slim, plump, going on strike for their rights."

Life magazine, in a big, four-page photo spread published after the strike was over, cast it as "Camp Woolworth": "The newest type of camping excur-sion is attended not by children of the rich but by members of the working classes. . . .Youngest, prettiest, most prevailingly feminine of such recent 'campers' were the 110 girls in Detroit's main Woolworth store who went on strike Feb. 27." The story continued with cute references to "camp duties," "camp equipment," and a "sit-down picnic" in Woolworth's "camping ground."

In account after account, the strikers were alleged to be obsessed with beauty. "Night and day one hundred girls occupy the closed store and primp-ing replaces clerking," intoned Pathé Newsreels. The strikers, the press noted, had set up their own beauty parlor in a corner of the store: "Everyone got a manicure and finger wave." *Life* assured, "A good appearance is maintained by Woolworth girls who comb their hair in the women's rest room and do not allow their camping excursion to interfere with their prinking [preening]."

The women were also supposed to be obsessed with boyfriends. The strike started on a Saturday, offering reporters the opportunity to focus on the all-important Saturday-night date as a threat to working-class solidarity. "Many girls wanted to leave the store because of a 'date with the boyfriend,' reported the *Detroit Times*. "These requests Miss Terral [sic] refused." A reporter for the *Detroit News* did a little eavesdropping on Saturday afternoon. "Gosh, I've got a date with my boy friend," a dark-haired girl named Mazie supposedly worried. "I can't reach him by telephone, either. He's going to think I'm standing him up."

These all-important dates allegedly produced the strike's only reported deserters. According to the *Detroit News*, "The first sign of any defection came at 3 p.m.," when Vita Terrall "discovered half a dozen girls deserted to keep Saturday night dates. They got out of the building through a basement door, through the assistance of two stock room boys, who were not on strike."

It's impossible to distinguish between what the Woolworth's strikers actually did and thought and how they were depicted. Clearly some of them were sincerely concerned about dates; but we only know that because reporters repeatedly brought the question up. We don't know if any of the Flint workers, for example, were just as worried about their own dates. We do know that the Woolworth's strikers themselves, on their second or third day, set up a "Love Booth." Boyfriends could enter the store and inhabit the booth for five minutes with their sweeties. (We are left imagining exactly what the couples might have accomplished in precisely five minutes.)

A favorite angle in the press was a little book called *How to Get Your Man and Hold Him*, with which, they insisted, the strikers were obsessed. A *Detroit News* photographer captured four women propped up on their stomachs on the floral-patterned mattresses, each reading a copy in what was clearly a posed shot. The *Detroit Times* reported that "a little huddle in one corner" had snatched up the book. "The girl who held the book was surrounded by others who pored over her shoulders and under her arms, intent on solving the problem." *Life* caught a photo of a huge, just-unwrapped pile of more than two hundred copies of the book—offering "Secrets of Flattery" for only ten cents—but conceded that "most of [the women] are sufficiently good-looking to make scholarly study of romantic technique unnecessary." One account claimed that the strikers had requested that the union buy them all copies, but it seems more plausible that Woolworth's simply had a large quantity in supply that day—another cheap, useful item.

In the media's eyes, then, the Woolworth's strikers were like Barbara Hutton: obsessed with beauty, makeup, hair, and fashion, and eager to parlay all four, along with a big dose of sparkle and flattery, to capture the man of their choice.

But of course it was all more complicated than that. The strikers were quite capable of manipulating the media right back. They were the ones who called Pathé Newsreels to come film them in the first place. The sleek, somber skirts and dressy, formal lace collars the clerks are wearing in press photos from Saturday might have been their regular work clothes, or the strikers may have dressed to the nines that morning, knowing full well they were about to be photographed by every paper in town. They definitely didn't wear high heels on normal work days. Once on strike the women read newspapers voraciously; discarded papers piled up in mountains in the aisles. The newspapers, in turn, ran photos of the strikers lined up at the lunch counter reading about themselves in the very same papers. The strikers were so conscious of the role of the media that one of the very first committees they set up was the Scrapbook Committee, to save all those stories about themselves. In other words, the women were both aware of media attention and able to employ it for their own ends, in part to buoy their spirits in what was, after all, a dicey situation.

Ironically, the "silly girls playing strike" media pitch gave the strikers power. It kept them on the front pages of the papers for days on end. Their very innocence legitimated their struggle. If these were just silly girls, why should Woolworth's exploit them? And if these were boy-crazy young things, just having a bit of fun in the aisles, it would certainly not look good at all if Woolworth's sent in the National Guard or thugs to drag them out by their carefully coiffed hair. Being cast as silly and a little stupid, in other words, protected them.

Being white girls protected them, too. Imagine the response if the strikers had been African American. Media sympathy for their plight as oppressed workers wouldn't have been in place beforehand—no Bing Crosby crooning hit songs that built up sympathy. Once on strike, police and public tolerance for their lawbreaking behavior would have been zero. Media interest outside the African American press would be mostly nonexistent or hostile. And *Life* would certainly not have shown up to depict them playing at Camp Woolworth.

If the Woolworth strikers' whiteness and their supposed silliness protected them, equally importantly, their beauty culture wasn't stupid at all. They knew that it was useful to powder their noses and put on a bit of lipstick before the reporters rushed in the door on Sunday morning. They took pleasure in making each other up and in looking good—that was why they set up a beauty parlor in the store. Photographs of the last day of their strike show them glowing, almost all with a set of beautiful curls, a bow in their hair, and a corsage, which, we can suspect, they had crafted from materials in the store during their occupation. Historian Kathy Peiss, in her wonderful study *Hope in a Jar*, has shown how savvy and artful working-class women were in their use of cosmetics. Women, she writes, deployed makeup "to declare themselves—to announce their adult status, sexual allure, youthful spirit, political beliefs—and even to proclaim the *right* to self-definition." Boys and sex could be fun, too. There was nothing wrong with wanting to go out on Saturday night for a kiss, a few well-placed squeezes, or maybe a lot more. And some of the women were in fact married.

"Getting a man and holding him" was in fact a smart economic strategy. Think about it: these were young working-class women in the depths of the

Great Depression. What were their choices? Stay single, stay in the labor force, join a union, go on strike, better their wages and working conditions— O.K., they were doing that. Or they could find a young man with a steady job and good wages, and marry him. In many ways that was the best choice available, and they knew it. They also knew that statistically, their chances of marriage had gotten slimmer and slimmer during the Depression. "We have no money to get married," one Woolworth clerk told a New York interviewer in 1939. "Unless Lady Luck comes along, we never will."

The very first page of *How to Get Your Man and Hold Him* only confirmed their choices: "No nice girl admits it out loud, but it is nevertheless true that there comes a time in every girl's life when she is seized with an urge to get married." The cause could be "strictly biological," or the urge could be caused by a Clark Gable movie, the author speculated, but it could also be caused by:

(a) The sudden realization that spinsterhood is just around the corner.
(b) The struggle to make both ends meet on one under-nourished pay envelope.
(c) Being fed up with the monotonous business of punching a time clock and writing letters.

Given the alternatives, in other words, it was smart to keep that date. Mazie needed to make that phone call or her boyfriend might think she was standing him up; she needed to paint her nails, or he might do a little shopping around himself.

Because they weren't, in fact, Barbara Hutton. She was rich, they were poor. She was rich *because* they were poor. These young women needed men for enormous economic reasons; Barbara Hutton had millions of her own and could buy a man by crooking her glittering little finger in his direction.

In their reports on the strike, labor and left-wing publications jumped on the contrast. The *Michigan Labor Paper* headlined an editorial "The Countess and the Counter Girl." The *Daily Worker*, in a story on the strike, ran a photograph not of the strikers themselves, but of Barbara Hutton. Best of all, the Woolworth's strikers made up wonderful songs about Hutton, and the press repeated them:

> Barbara Hutton's got the dough, parlez vous.
> We know where she got it, too, parlez vous.
> We slave at Woolworth's five-and-dime,
> The pay we get is sure a crime. Hinky dinky parlez vous.

Some of the women working at Woolworth's that first morning may have decided hanging on to their men was in fact more important than striking— hence the basement-door deserters, although there were plenty of other reasons for skipping out. But the majority of the women tried to mediate between the two strategies, to make striking and seducing compatible. "Sure I love you," one striker assures someone on the phone in a newsreel, "but we're sticking right here until we win." We don't really know: maybe their sweeties were militant union activists who loved them all the more because they were on strike.

Many of the strikers leapt to enforce solidarity among the ranks lest their sisters waver. Not only did Vita Terrall police the doors, but on that Saturday night, when "some of the girls thought of their dates and tried to get out," according to the *Detroit News*, "Mae, of the sodas... just stuck her gum in the locks on the back doors. Those doors are locked for keeps." When Mazie, quoted earlier, allegedly lamented she couldn't get ahold of her boyfriend, "'Forget it,' said her blond next-door neighbor, Sally. "Don't you suppose he'll hear about this? . . . And anyhow . . . this is more important than your boyfriend. We've got to win this strike."

Defections aside, the women's beauty culture could also support their sense of community and solidarity. They had a lot of time to kill; they could bond by sharing tips on curling irons and clever flattery; they could keep themselves distracted by making out with boyfriends in that Love Booth; they could imagine a happy married future... and not worry about what the outcome of their strike might be.

In the rare instances we have in which the Woolworth's strikers spoke to the public directly, they didn't mention beautification at all but articulated the concrete reasons for their sit-down. "All we want is a living wage," they said, in big red crayon letters on pieces of cardboard and brown wrapping paper they put in the front windows facing the street. In Pathé's first newsreel of the strike, a woman in her twenties with brown hair, carefully pencilled arched eyebrows, glossy lipstick, and a striped cotton top says to the camera, very seriously: "We have the best food that anyone could ask for, and when we get our union, we hope that it will be recognized throughout all the retail stores so as to give us shorter hours and living wages. I thank you." She made a little bow, and smiled. She was probably Vita Terrall.

And there were other ways to resolve the contradiction between striking and seducing. The Love Booth aside, the strikers were, after all, having a great time without men. Once Loew and Mayer moved upstairs, the strike was one big endless all-female slumber party of indeterminate duration. The women did each other's nails and hair with loving affection and danced with their arms around each other's waists. If you watch Pathé's first newsreel carefully, you can catch one of the strikers reaching over to tickle the back of the woman next to her.

Sunday night, they tucked themselves in and dreamed sugary dreams of sweethearts, Barbara Hutton, and a living wage.

WOOLWORTH STRIKE ESCALATES AS UNIONS CLOSE SECOND STORE

The strikers were having a great time, but the purpose of their strike wasn't to guarantee they had lots of fun; the goal, after all, was to get Woolworth's management to give in on wages, hours of work, and a sea of other demands. While all that dancing was going on Sunday, the situation hadn't moved toward a resolution one whit. By Monday, March 1, two days had passed and Woolworth's hadn't budged an inch.

So on Monday, the unions escalated the situation dramatically, heightening the pressure on the Woolworth's managers and raising the stakes for everyone involved.

On Saturday afternoon, Louis Koenig had evidently threatened to close all forty Woolworth's stores in Detroit, with their thousand employees. A bluff, maybe? Sometime on Monday in the morning or early afternoon, officials of the cooks', waiters', and retail clerks' unions had a private meeting downtown. Then, at 3:00, Mira Komaroff and other folks from the three unions drove down Woodward Avenue to a second, smaller Woolworth's store at 6565 Grand Boulevard, just off Woodward. They met briefly with a few of the twenty-six women who worked as clerks and waitresses there. At 3:30 sharp, Mira yelled out, "Strike! Strike!" and eleven women stopped working. "There was no disorder as the clerks who did not desire to participate donned wraps and left," reported the *Daily Worker*. "The striking girls clustered about the soda fountain, talking with the union organizers. Customers departed, doors were locked." Mira and the other officials bought "a supply of food at the lunch counter with which to feed the strikers." Then they asked all the managers to leave. "There was no violence," reported the *Detroit Times*, once again. And now a second Woolworth's store was occupied by striking women.

Now the unions' threats to escalate the strike to all forty stores in Detroit looked a whole lot more serious. Monday night, Louis Koenig cast his own ultimatum back at Woolworth's, upping the ante still further: "Unless the strike here is settled within a week of the time it started [i.e., by Saturday, March 6]," he proclaimed, "I will ask the executive council of our association to call a national sit down"—thus closing all the Woolworth's stores in the country.

Local solidarity in support of the strikers at both stores shot up. A formal system of picketing outside kicked in. During the next few days "nearly every hotel worker in the downtown area found their way to the Woolworth store to wish the women luck," Loew recalled. One visitor was Paul Domeney, an immigrant from Transylvania who worked as a room service waiter at the Book-Cadillac luxury hotel in downtown Detroit at the time, and was active as a leftist within the waiters' union. Together with Mira Komaroff he visited the picket line and even went inside the store to talk with the strikers and help shore up their spirits. Homer Martin, national president of the United Auto Workers, came in and gave a big pep talk, pledging his union's ongoing support.

Local Detroit activists like Paul Domeney, Mira Komaroff, and Floyd Loew assiduously sought to evade the growing national split between the jurassic AFL and the upstart CIO. While conflict between the two titans turned increasingly nasty on the national level, unionists on the ground in Detroit tried hard to keep working together in the interests of solidarity. "Our unions are AFL affiliates but we are working peaceably with [the] CIO," Mira Komaroff went out of her way to insist to the press. The waiters' and waitresses' union, affiliated nationally with the Hotel Employees and Restaurant Employees' International Union, was, on the one hand, still an AFL union, as were the retail clerks. The United Auto Workers, on the other hand, was the quintessential CIO affiliate, challenging AFL craft jurisdictions as handily as it had taken on General Motors. Frank Martel, president of the Detroit and Wayne County Federation of Labor, emerged as a rare figure in this period, trying to bridge the gap between CIO and AFL. He not only showed up at the Woolworth's strike downtown the minute it broke out, but on Monday carefully told the press that "the local Federation would have been inadequate to handle the appeals of strikers had not the automobile union lent assistance."

Throughout the country, unions, working people, and their allies rushed to express their support for the Woolworth's strikers. Edward Flore, national president of HERE, announced that he would arrive in Detroit on the next Monday, March 8. Telegrams flooded in from Chicago, Philadelphia, Boston, New York, and all over, both to the Woolworth's strikers directly and to the national offices of HERE and the retail clerks' union. Someone named W.J. Boenckleman, from New Orleans, sent a telegram saying he held thirty shares of Woolworth's stock and was "100% with the sitdowners in their efforts to enforce demands." The strikers plastered their telegrams all over the store's ground-floor windows for all to see.

Supporters also sent cash to support the strikers, who needed money for food, supplies, and to replace the earnings they were forgoing with every passing day. Vita Terrall announced on Monday that the AFL had donated a thousand dollars. Union staffers assured the press that the strikers had been guaranteed enough funds "to continue the strike indefinitely," with money promised from Chicago, New York, and other cities.

The unions did everything they could to publicize all this support, to signal to Woolworth's that they were invincible. But at the same time, in private, they were doing everything they could to create a way out for the corporation by setting up possible avenues for mediation. Throughout Monday and Tuesday rumors floated all over town that either the Detroit Board of Commerce or the Detroit Retail Merchants Association would be mediating a settlement.

But for all that, Woolworth's didn't move—or so it seemed.

Think about the situation from Woolworth's point of view. Its managers were caught between a rock of solidarity and a very expensive place. Unlike the "girls," they were not happy campers, and with every passing play day, they got less happy.

Who exactly was "Woolworth's" anyway? Ultimately, the corporation rested in the hands of its stockholders who, in 1937, included Frank Woolworth's heirs, the company's longtime upper-level managers and their heirs, and those who had bought its stock in later decades. In practice, an elaborate chain of command stretched upward and outward from local managers like Frank Mayer. When the strike started on Saturday morning, Mayer called his own boss, Dahlquist, the Detroit area manager—the man who issued the ultimatum at the top of the stairs that afternoon. Dahlquist, in turn, had called O. L. Gause, of Woolworth's regional headquarters in Cleveland. But even Gause wasn't really in charge; he then answered to the executives in the Woolworth's building in New York City. All these men—and they were all men—answered to Charles Deyo, the company's president.

The very elaborateness and length of this chain of command, combined with the firm's geographic dispersal in an era of expensive long-distance phone calls, slowed down the negotiation process immensely. This was no quickie, no three-hour tour, unlike so many of the dozens of sit-down strikes in Detroit the week before, in part because it took more than three hours for communication to move up, let alone back down, the chain of command.

The big shots in New York did every thing they could to act like indifferent power figures at an omnipotent corporation swatting away the Detroit sit-downers like pesky flies. On Monday, after the occupation of the second store began, Edward P. Houbert, a lawyer for the company, insisted, "Our attitude is still the same—we will not bargain, as long as strikers remain in the stores." Company vice president E. C. Mauchly "telegraphed from New York that the strike was a local incident and would have to be handled through the district headquarters at Cleveland," *Women's Wear Daily* reported.

But Woolworth's bigness also meant that the stakes were higher. If the company gave in and granted the strikers' demands, it would cost a lot of money—not just in wages at the two stores on strike, but in the other forty Detroit stores as well. The stores' profits would drop and perhaps the company's stock price would plummet as well.

The managers had no way of knowing, moreover, if a small—but very public—settlement with the unions in Detroit would lead to organizing efforts and sit-down strikes at their stores all over the country, or even in Canada, Great Britain, Germany, or Cuba. More broadly, they would have been deeply hostile, ideologically, to unions, especially the militant kind that occupied their property and held them hostage. They had a stake in drawing the line against the national upsurge of union activism under way, and some among them might even have been a little bit worried about a social revolution.

Much as it might have wanted to uphold its own version of corporate class solidarity during the Depression, Woolworth's also had to keep looking over its shoulder at its competitors. A settlement might disrupt its position in relation to the other variety stores snapping at the heels of its market share, in particular S.S. Kresge—headquartered, coincidentally, in Detroit. Kresge itself, watching the sit-down handwriting on its own wall that Saturday, raised the wages of its own Detroit workers from fourteen to seventeen dollars a week within five *hours* of the Woolworth's strike. Kresge's thus cleverly averted any labor action in its own stores, plus it enjoyed the nice side benefit of being open while Woolworth's was closed.

Last but not least, the public relations pressures on Woolworth's were enormous. The movement against "the chain store menace" was at its peak. It was the Great Depression, and here was a giant corporation exploiting innocent young white women. And of course, with their songs and pickets, the strikers themselves kept reminding the public of the self-indulgent Barbara Hutton. Polls revealed that public opinion largely supported the new sit-down strikes. Working-class people were especially enthusiastic. And they shopped at Woolworth's—or at least they had before the strike.

Woolworth's had three basic choices: one, settle; two, hold out and see if the strikers would give up; or three, send in the police. The armed solution was a real option. All the company had to do was get a judge to issue an injunction against the strikers on trespassing charges and in theory it would be able to call upon the Detroit police or the National Guard to evict the strikers forcibly. That same Saturday another strike had erupted at the Ferro Stamping Company in Detroit, and by Tuesday its owners had obtained an injunction. The strikers had left the plant voluntarily, defeated. But not all judges would comply, and for a brief time in February and March, both the mayor of Detroit and Governor Frank Murphy were unwilling to send in troops to evict sit-downers—that was one reason why the General Motors strikers had won. The *Detroit Free Press* reported on Sunday that A. J. Dahlquist had "indicated that police action to gain evacuation was contemplated," but it seems to have been an empty threat. We have no other evidence that Woolworth's ever considered a forcible solution. Again, to do so would have been a spectacular public relations fiasco; all those nasty cops, all those manicured nails.

Clearly the strikers, when lined up in solidarity with all their allies all over the country, held enormous power over the corporation. Notice just one detail: when the women occupying the second store asked their own bosses to leave the store, the men filed out like obedient sheep.

But that didn't mean victory. It just meant that Woolworth's was feeling the heat.

SIT-DOWNS SPREAD IN AREA HOTELS; WILL SEND FUNDS, SAY NEW YORK UNIONS

Tuesday, March 2. Day four of the Woolworth's strike. National solidarity ratcheted up another big notch. The executive committee of the big, radical Local #1250 of the Retail Clerks' International Protective Association in New York met that night, then dispatched a telegram of ringing support: "Congratulations courageous Woolworth workers. Notify us how we can cooperate." They had already planned a big dance for the coming Saturday night at the Savoy Ballroom, at 140th and Lenox Avenue, to benefit the Loyalist cause in the Spanish Civil War. On Tuesday night they voted to donate 25 percent of the take to their sisters in Detroit. Most importantly, the union was planning a demonstration for that same Saturday, March 6, which, it announced in a national press release, "will open a boycott of the Woolworth stores in New York pending the outcome of the strike." To keep the pressure on, a delegation from several local unions would call on Woolworth executives to notify them officially of the planned boycott and "urge granting of the Detroit demands." Hinting at future direct action of their own, the retail clerks' union also issued a statement that working conditions in New York City "were as bad or worse than those in Detroit."

By now people all over the country had been following the story for days. The papers had headlined the story since Saturday, the newsreels were now in the movie theaters, and regular working folks had had time to think about what the women were doing. The Communist Party's *Daily Worker,* based in New York, sent reporter Louise Mitchell out to check on what local Woolworth's workers had to say about their sisters in Detroit. "The slight, undernourished counter girl in a crisp white collar" who worked at the "wash cloth counter" confided, "Everyone is talking about it. . . . Everyone who comes in. . . . There's something going on all right." She was no dummy about cause and effect, either: "Everybody is sitting down. If you want something you just take a squat and they come to terms." At a different variety store, "over the sandwich counter," "a fair platinum haired girl" told Mitchell, "I'd like to sit right down now and do I wish I was there. If we ever did it in New York . . . they'd have a job to combat it." The "girl" behind the stationery counter agreed: "Wait till this thing comes to New York. Of course it'll come.

We're all watching them and not saying much."

Closer to home, the lid burst off the top of labor activism in Detroit. Thousands of local workers had also had a few days to contemplate what the Woolworth's women were doing and be inspired themselves. Now service workers in downtown Detroit as well as factory workers suddenly sat down. Tuesday, at Stouffer's, sixty waitresses and kitchen workers occupied their restaurant at the middle of the lunchtime rush. Workers at Huyler's Cafeteria in the Fisher Building sat down at the same time, then barricaded the doors.

For every actual sit-down, hundreds of employers fearful of potential strikes raised their workers' wages, as had S.S. Kresge. Again, the mere threat of a strike produced swift results. "More wage increases have been made effective within the past few days by local stores," reported *Women's Wear Daily* on Tuesday, "in anticipation of projected unionization efforts.... There are various rumors cropping up regarding sit-down strikes in other local stores, but none have developed." That same day Anthony A.Henk, secretary of the Detroit Retail Merchants Association, "announced that about 800 clerks in 450 meat shops and groceries would receive immediate wage increases averaging 5 percent."

"Brothers, we've got 'em on the run!" exulted the *Detroit Labor News* that week. But it didn't bode well that the *Labor News* wrote the sisters out of labor's success story so quickly; indeed, by Tuesday the focus of stories about Detroit activism had begun to move away from the Woolworth's strikers. New strikes bumped them off the front page, and soon most papers reduced them to a tiny side reference in a general labor story or dropped them altogether.

The new hotel and restaurant strikes in downtown Detroit, moreover, siphoned off the organizing support of Louis Koenig, Mira Komaroff, Floyd Loew, and other union staffers, who now spent their days helping with other efforts. Mary Davis, a rank-and-file union waitress at the time, remembers going down to pay a solidarity visit at Woolworth's on Monday or Tuesday, as a fellow member of Local 705. The picket line was small, she recalls—maybe thirty people. Five or six of the picketers were left-wing activists like herself, but the rest were very depressed and discouraged Woolworth's strikers, all of them women in their twenties or thirties who weren't inside because of family commitments or because they hadn't been at work the day the strike began. They told Mary that the strikers weren't getting very much support from the union, and that they were very worried.

We don't know much about exactly what was going on within the store on Tuesday or the next day, precisely because the press had by and large moved on to other stories. *Life* magazine showed up on one of these days, and while it captured the two women sliding down banisters in their funny playsuits, other women they spoke to admitted to being bored. We can only wonder if everyone was getting along after all that time in close quarters together. One woman photographed by *Life* had abandoned the three-person mattresses on the floor and made a bed for herself on a countertop. By mid-week the women had exhausted the store's supply of sanitary napkins, and new supplies had to be brought in. At some point during the occupation, one woman miscarried.

Would they really be able to manage all the logistics necessary to hold out as days stretched into weeks? As a rule, the longer a strike, the more likely it is to be lost. Usually it's either a quick victory within hours or a day, or a long, extended, painful exhaustion of resources, spirits, and public interest, chipping away slowly at solidarity and the workers' power. By now, the first flush of excitement over and press attention waning, the Woolworth's strikers would have had plenty of time to think about what would happen if they lost: they'd certainly lose a week's pay, likely lose their jobs, and maybe even be blacklisted by Detroit's other stores and restaurants. The families of the single women might be rock-solid behind them, or they might be increasingly irritated that they weren't around to help wash the dishes or watch their little brothers at night. The husbands of married strikers might be home patching together meals in proud solidarity, or they might be getting impatient, even angry. And those boyfriends—rather than holding their men, some of the strikers might be letting them slip away.

If they lost the strike, moreover, the negative ripple effects would be immense. And despite all that glorious solidarity and the upsurge of new strikes, Woolworth's still hadn't budged. Tuesday came and went. O. L. Gause, the company's regional supervisor in Cleveland, said only that they were "surveying the situation" in Detroit. "That's all there is to it," he snapped curtly.

STEELMAKERS CAPITULATE TO CIO IN BIG AGREEMENT

Wednesday, March 4. Sort of like a good news, bad news routine. Seemingly out of the blue, U.S. Steel, reaching its own conclusions from the General Motors strike, gave in to the CIO's Steel Workers' Organizing Committee and signed a huge national agreement recognizing the union, granting an eight-hour day and a forty-hour week and raising wages by 10 percent. It was stunning news, a huge and total victory for the CIO. And it bumped the Woolworth's story out of the papers altogether.

But that same Wednesday, Woolworth's, in its first concession, granted a wage increase to thirty-five women who worked in the restaurant of one of its Boston stores. Some full-time workers got free meals "for the first time in the store's history." With delicious obsequiousness, Woolworth's managers first told the women of the increases, then begged, "Remember, now, no sit-down strike."

NEGOTIATIONS BEGIN IN STORE STAY-INS

Then, finally, the company began to cave. On Wednesday night, Woolworth's executives met for the first time in negotiations with the Detroit Woolworth's unions. They parleyed again on Thursday, in the office of Frank Bostroff, secretary of the Michigan Restauranteurs' Association, who served as mediator. On the workers' side were Louis Koenig, from the waiters' and waitresses' union, Louis Walters, from the cooks', and Louis Salter, from the retail clerks'. *Women's Wear Daily* reported that the identity of the Woolworth's representatives had "been guarded closely since they came to Detroit," but that "it is understood that they are vice presidents in charge of operation from the New York City office." The men were eventually revealed to be A. F. Weber, superintendent of the Midwest region, and John R. Powers and H. W. Frank, the rumored vice presidents. The choice of representatives is telling on both sides. Woolworth's thought that this strike was important enough to send in big shots from New York, while the women whose action had forced them to do that didn't even get to be present at the discussions negotiating their own strike settlement.

All day, contradictory rumors flew about as to the progress of the negotiations. One report confided that Woolworth's was "known to favor a settlement before the end of the week." Another cited "reliable sources" as saying that the company was "willing to grant practically all of the wage demands of the strikers, but is considering the possible effect on other stores throughout the country before making [a] decision"—that is, they too were worried about the ripple effect, especially, rumor had it, a settlement's effect on the retail clerks' union.

Friday morning, *Women's Wear Daily* reported that "observers who were inclined to the belief that an early settlement would be reached when negotiations started are less optimistic today."

STRIKE AT DIME STORES ENDS WITH BIG WAGE BOOST

All day Friday they talked. Then, at 5:30 PM on Friday, March 5, the strike's seventh day, just in time to avert Koenig's Saturday deadline for expanding the strike and to avoid the boycott in New York, Woolworth's and the unions announced they had reached an agreement.

No question, it was an absolute and clear-cut victory for the strikers. They won an entire laundry list of demands, including the laundry. First, the company agreed to a five-cent an hour increase for all female employees—a 20 to 25 percent raise, depending on each woman's previous rate. New employees would start at $14.50 a week for the first six months. Everyone would get time and a half for overtime, after a forty-eight-hour work week. Future workers would be hired through the unions' offices. Uniforms would be furnished and laundered by the company for free. The vacation schedule would stay the same.

Notices of union meetings could be posted on bulletin boards in the women's locker room and bathrooms. And, most amazing of all, the women would be paid at 50 percent of their usual rate for the time they were occupying the store (though not, presumably, for twenty-four-hour days). Without ever striking, the cooks (who were all male) also got a wage increase and shorter working hours. Moreover, the agreement covered not just the two stores that had been taken over, but all forty Woolworth's stores in the city.

Woolworth's got almost nothing in return, just a little clause saying union employees couldn't coerce nonunion coworkers. It did its feeble best to look strong. "The increase in salaries granted to employees in the two Woolworth stores which had sit-down strikes is not to be store-wide," its executives insisted. In a classic pitch for containment, they declared that "each district is operated in accordance with conditions prevailing in that particular sector, and all matters of policy are determined by the regional supervisor."

Needless to say, once the strikers heard of the agreement, they were ecstatic. The women from the second store quickly packed up their things and rushed down to the main store. Then all the women "sang and cheered Vita Terrall, the strike leader, until 8:30, the evacuation deadline." In between they posed for photographers on the big main staircase, holding up giant cardboard letters on sticks that spelled out "WE WON." Over a thousand people—friends, family, "curious onlookers"—jammed the sidewalks outside, cheering and clapping. "The women then marched by twos carrying their grips and bedding," waving American flags and singing, reported the *Detroit Free Press*, in a "victory parade" down to the Lindbergh Room at the Barium Hotel. Along the way more onlookers cheered and applauded. Once they were all in the room, Koenig read the agreement out loud to the strikers and he and Walters and Salter signed it officially. (None of the striking women got to vote to approve the agreement, or to sign it.) Then an array of speakers stepped forth to congratulate them, including Frances Comfort from the schoolteachers' union, who'd addressed the strikers on their very first day, and Larry Davidow, a lawyer for the UAW. It was a great moment.

On Saturday Woolworth's announced a special sale.

STRIKE SENTIMENT RAMPANT;
CHAIN STORE ORGANIZATION FLOURISHES;
BABS RENOUNCES CITIZENSHIP BUT NOT PROFITS

We don't know what the women did next. But we do know that in the aftermath of their victory, its ripple effects swept through the nation's stores and restaurants for over a year.

The first wave engulfed Detroit. Clerks at the twelve-story Crowley-Milner department store downtown sat down, and after three days won a wage raise, the five-day, forty-hour week, and union recognition. Workers at Federated Department Stores won in a few hours. At Lerner's, it took three days, and by the end of the week three shoe stores had joined in too. Those were just the big shops. "I would be in the local union office and a girl would call up suddenly," Mira Komaroff recalled, "saying 'Say, is this Myra? [sic] Someone told me to call you. I'm Mamie, over in Liggett's Drug Store. We threw out the manager, chased out the customers and closed up the place. We are "sitting in." What should we do *now*?'"

By the middle of March, other Mamies all over the country were sitting down in the wake of the Woolworth's victory. In New York, workers struck five H. L. Green department stores on March 13. Then the retail clerks' union, just as they had hinted the week before, took on Woolworth's. This time the situation got much dicier. On March 17, forty of seventy workers at the store on 34th Street declared a sit-down strike, but in this case the remaining clerks kept working, so the managers soon reopened the store to customers. Undaunted, "throughout the day, at regular intervals, the strikers snake-danced through the store, chanting 'We're on strike.'" When the managers locked the doors at the end of the day, the women stayed in for the night. To sneak in food and bedding, their allies made a human chain to haul it all up through a second-story window. On the second day police evicted the strikers, but they marched right back in again, and this time took up their usual positions behind the counters and just stood there, not speaking or helping customers. Arrests, skirmishes, and picketing multiplied for days, until finally Mayor Fiorello LaGuardia agreed to mediate. The strikers won a six-month contract granting union recognition, wage increases, a grievance system, time and a half for overtime, and vacations with pay—for all twenty-five hundred Woolworth's workers in the city.

These New York strikers were directly inspired by their Detroit sisters. "DETROIT STRIKERS WIN!! . . . WE CAN WIN TOO! JOIN THE UNION," a leaflet passed out before the strike exhorted. May Brooks, a Communist organizer at the time, captured wonderfully in an oral history both the improvisational character of the sitdowns that erupted in New York and the importance of Detroit and other precedents: "So there we were, and we didn't know what we were going to do, once we blew the whistle—you know, what to expect and with no experience—just feeling this was . . . the tactic now, and . . . this could work. And of course, we'd read and heard about other sit-down strikes that were beginning to take place . . . and were tremendous."

The New Yorkers were even quicker than the Detroit women to drag in poor Barbara Hutton. In one clever organizing leaflet distributed before the New York strike, activists told the mythical story of "Little Barbara Button" who worked at the "Millworks" store at "35th and Wiseway." They devised even better slogans—"Barbara Hutton eats good mutton. Woolworth workers they get nuttin'"—and even appealed directly to the heiress herself in a telegram sent during the strike. Alas, Hutton, having recently purchased a set of emeralds for $1.2 million, was off on a sightseeing tour in the Sahara atop a camel and never responded. Allegedly her new husband pocketed the missive when it arrived and she never saw it.

In December, the "Babs vs. Woolworth girls" plot thickened. That fall, the retail clerks' union in New York went on to achieve success after success, organizing five thousand new workers by the year's end. But when the Woolworth's contract expired at the end of October, the company refused to renew it. Smack in the middle of increasing publicity about the situation, on December 15 Barbara Hutton Mdivani Haugwitz-Reventlow sailed into New York harbor and stopped in town just long enough to sign papers renouncing her American citizenship so she could save four hundred thousand dollars a year in taxes (she had gained Danish citizenship automatically when she married Reventlow). Barbara's public image plummeted to an all-time low.

The press was relentless. "The shopgirls . . . have been contributing their mites toward [Barbara's] income of $2,000,000 a year," charged Scripps-Howard columnist Westbrook Pegler, "without which their own 'princess' might never have aroused the love of her ideal. Now she has betrayed them for all time."

Woolworth's activists played it to the hilt, launching a new strike three days later. Workers and their allies paraded up and down sidewalks all over town wearing sandwich boards: "BABS RENOUNCES CITIZENSHIP BUT NOT PROFITS." "WHILE WE STRIKE FOR HIGHER PAY, BABS TAKES HER MONEY AND RUNS AWAY." Once again, they telegrammed Barbara: "URGE THAT YOU ORDER MANAGEMENT TO CONCEDE A LIVING WAGE TO THOUSANDS NOW EXISTING ON STARVATION WAGES." She never responded, but Woolworth's executives settled the strike after its first day. As of July 1938, *Life* was still haunting Barbara. It ran a photo of her "wearing richly embroidered Oriental beach pajamas," with the admonition, "She should forget counts who spend her money and remember the Woolworth girls who earn it."

These organizing successes in New York and Detroit were only a few examples of a nationwide uprising of store clerks that year. Frances Comfort, the Detroit teacher, had been right: the strikers had indeed been fighting not only for themselves but for thousands like themselves all over the country. "The situation in Detroit has thoroughly aroused the salespeople everywhere," wrote the retail clerks' national magazine in April. "Retail management is finally aroused to a fuller sense of responsibility and realization that employees are people, not merely groups of automatons, to be herded and managed without regard to human rights and ambitions." The next month they put it even better: "Since the action of the Detroit employees in February, Woolworth and other variety store employees in a number of cities are rebelling against the inhibitions of enforced paternalism that these employers have used in the past to keep their employees loyal to the firm instead of loyal to themselves and fellow workers."

In the third week of March 1937, picketing in East St. Louis produced a single union contract covering workers at Woolworth's, Grant's, Newberry's, and Kresge stores across the entire city, and a brief strike won a union and increases for workers at four chains in Akron, Ohio. In May, workers in St. Louis got a contract covering fifteen hundred workers at thirty-three Woolworth's stores. That summer victories proliferated like glorious poppies across the national landscape, spreading from variety stores to grocery store chains to department stores—in St. Paul, Minnesota; in Centralia, Washington; in Superior, Wisconsin. By the year's end, Tacoma, San Francisco, and Duluth had joined the list, along with Seattle, where three thousand clerks in twenty-three stores, including Sears, J. C. Penney, Frederick & Nelson's, the Bon Marche, and Lerner's, won not only the forty-hour week but a pay increase "estimated to increase the income of the employees by at least one half-million dollars." More than sixty years later, unions today in department stores all over the country owe their existence in part to the Woolworth's strike.

Last but not least, the Woolworth's strike lived on in popular culture. *Pins and Needles*, a new Broadway musical, opened in November of 1938 with a catchy tune, "Chain Store Daisy," about the grievances of a Vassar student laboring at a department store. Two years later, Jean Arthur, Charles Coburn, and Robert Cummings starred in the screwball comedy *The Devil and Miss Jones*, which featured a mean department store owner who goes underground as a salesclerk to break a union at his own store, but, when a strike breaks out, ends up converted to the workers' cause.

DAVID TRIUMPHS OVER GOLIATH IN STUNNING UPSET

All this from a hundred and eight very young, entirely ordinary young women who one day in Detroit decided to stage a sit-down. That was the brilliance of it—it wasn't some mythical superheroes who had pulled it off, but regular young women with no experience of striking, let alone of occupying a major chain store twenty-four hours a day for seven long days. They took on one of the biggest corporate powers of their time and won big, inspiring hundreds of thousands of other ordinary salesclerks—and who knows who else—to stand up (or sit down) for their rights, to claim a living wage, to demand an end to corporate paternalism, and to insist they were indeed live and vibrant human beings, not change-making machines. They danced and made up songs and did each others' nails and slid down banisters precisely because they were alive and knew it and wanted more from life than fifty-four hours a week of subservience in painful shoes. And they taught the arrogant Woolworth's corporation an enormous lesson.

In retrospect, what they did looks simple, almost easy. But they could easily have lost, and they won because they had an enormous array of powers behind them: the example of the General Motors workers, the force of public opinion, neutrality from the mayor and governor, spectacular solidarity from thousands of allies, and, best of all, their own sense of audacity, of fun, and of faith in themselves.

What's the lesson? With enough allies, with enough inspiration, and with enough daring, anything can happen.

Epilogue

Louis Koenig, a.k.a. "Smiley," stayed on as secretary-treasurer of Local 705, the Detroit waiters' and waitresses' union. He retired in 1960 at the age of seventy-two and spent the rest of his life at a nursing home in Florida.

Mira Komaroff stayed on at Local 705 too, first as recording secretary and then, after Koenig retired in 1960, inheriting his job as secretary-treasurer. In 1939 she married and changed her name to Myra Wolfgang. She went on to become an international vice president of the Hotel Employees and Restaurant Employees International Union in 1952 and a pioneer woman leader in the AFL-CIO, fighting for equal pay and the minimum wage, and helping to found CLUW, the Coalition of Labor Union Women, in 1974. She died of a brain tumor in 1976, a month before her sixty-second birthday.

Floyd Loew was purged from the local in 1943, after he refused to cooperate with Koenig and Komaroff/Wolfgang and cross a picket line during a strike at Harper Hospital in Detroit. He remained active as a dissident rank-and-file activist in HERE for the rest of his life, in Florida, Las Vegas, and Los Angeles. He died in the mid-1990s.

Paul Domeney, the Hungarian waiter, and *Mary Davis*, the union waitress, who both visited the picket line during the Woolworth's strike, were purged from Local 705 in the fall of 1938 for advocating rank-and-file participation in contract negotiations, the right of rank-and-filers to vote on ratification of their own contracts, and one unified union of all restaurant workers. Domeney lost his job at the Book-Cadillac Hotel as a result and was blacklisted from work in the city's hotels and restaurants. In 1940 he founded an independent union of Detroit restaurant workers, Local 1064, affiliated with the CIO, which survives to this day. He retired to Florida in 1999 at the age of ninety. Mary Davis is still thriving as an independent activist for social justice in Detroit.

In April, 1937, Governor Frank Murphy and other officials cracked down on sit-down strikes in Detroit. Throughout the nation, state and local governments moved swiftly to restore private property rights at the point of a gun, ending the sit-down wave. But the *Congress of Industrial Organizations* nonetheless went on to greater and greater victories throughout the late

1930s and the 1940s. By 1948 it represented almost four and a half million workers in industries all over the country. In 1955, the CIO merged with the AFL to form the AFL-CIO.

The *Woolworth Corporation* continued to expand during the 1940s and 1950s. In February of 1960, a new wave of young people launched sit-ins at its stores throughout the South to protest the chain's refusal to serve African Americans at its lunch counters. Protesters joined them to picket Woolworth's stores throughout the country. The chain finally agreed to serve African Americans, and eventually hired them to work in its stores as well.

Although the Woolworth Corporation acquired new subchains such as Foot Locker and Kinney Shoes and grew to 6,700 stores by 1996, the company failed to keep up with new megastores such as Wal-Mart and Costco in the 1980s and 1990s. In 1997 it reorganized itself as the Venator Corporation and closed all its Woolworth's stores throughout the United States. With the exception of two boxes of photographs of the Woolworth Building, all its records are destroyed or lost, and Woolworth's no longer exists.

Barbara Hutton divorced Kurt Haugwitz-Reventlow in 1941 and went on to marry five more times, to Cary Grant, Prince Igor Troubetzkoy, Porfirio Rubirosa, Baron Gottfried Von Cramm, and Prince Raymond Doan Vinh Na Champassak. She died of anorexia in 1979, at the age of sixty-six.

The *Hotel Employees and Restaurant Employees International Union*, of which Detroit Local 705 was part, became one of the most progressive and dynamic unions in the country, winning organizing drives in the 1980s and 1990s at Yale University, Las Vegas casinos, and hotels throughout downtown Los Angeles. In 2001 it represented 250,000 workers and was known for its commitment to union democracy, interracial solidarity, and worker militance.

The *Detroit Woolworth's workers* lost their union contract when it came up for renewal in October of 1937. As individual women left the store, management deliberately replaced them with anti-union workers who didn't then fight to keep the union.

The names of the strikers themselves are lost to the historical record, and we don't know what they did with the rest of their lives. Some of them, presumably, Got Their Man and Held Him. Some of them didn't. Some of them did other things altogether.

Bibliography

For the history of Woolworth's, start with James Brough, *The Woolworths* (New York: McGraw-Hill, 1982). See also Robert C. Kirkwood, *The Woolworth Story at Home and Abroad* (New York: Newcomen Society, 1960); John P. Nichols, *Skyline Queen and the Merchant Prince* (New York, Trident Press, 1973); John K. Winkler, *Five and Ten: The Fabulous Life of F. W. Woolworth* (New York: Robert McBride, 1940); *F. W. Woolworth at Ninety: Diversified for Dominance* (Orange, Conn.: Lebhar-Friedman, 1968); Alan R. Raucher, "Dime Store Chains: The Making of Organization Men, 1880-1940," *Business History Review* 65 (spring 1991): 130-63; Adele Hast, ed., *International Directory of Company Histories* (Detroit: St. James Press, 1992, 1998), vol. 5, 224-27; vol. 20, 528-32; Annual Reports, F. W. Woolworth Company, 1912-1950; regular articles in *Chain Store Age* during the 1920s and 1930s.

On Barbara Hutton, the best source is C. David Heymann, *Poor Little Rich Girl: The Life and Legend of Barbara Hutton* (Seacaucus, N.J.: L. Stuart, 1984); see also Brough, *The Woolworths*. Other sources include Dean Jennings, *Barbara Hutton: A Candid Biography* (New York: Frederick Fell, 1968); and Philip Van Rensselaer, *Million Dollar Baby: An Intimate Portrait of Barbara Hutton* (New York: Putnam, 1979). For a wonderful analysis of cosmetics, beautification, and women's appropriation of both, consult Kathy Peiss, *Hope in a Jar: The Making of America's Beauty Culture* (New York: Henry Holt, 1998). For tips, *How to Get Your Man and Hold Him*, illustrated by Dorothy Hoover Downs (A. L. Taylor, 1936), is still widely available in stores that sell used and rare books.

On the growth of chain stores—including additional material on Woolworth's—the literature is vast. A sampling includes Godfrey M. Lebhar, *Chain Stores in America, 1859-1962*, third ed. (New York: Chain Store Publishing Co., 1963); Charles G. Daughters, *Wells of Discontent: A Study of the Economic, Social, and Political Aspects of the Chain Store* (New York: Newson & Co., 1937); William J. Baxter, *Chain Store Distribution and Management* (New York: Harper & Bros., 1928); John Peter Nichols, *The Chain Store Tells Its Story* (New York: Institute of Distribution, 1940); Raucher, "Dime Store Chains"; Thomas Mahoney and Leonard Sloane, *The Great Merchants:*

America's Foremost Retail Institutions and the People Who Made Them Great (New York: Harper & Row, 1966); Joseph Gustaitis, "The Nickel and Dime Empire," *American History* 33, no. 1 (1998): 40-46.

For the anti-chain movement, see Carl G. Ryant, "The Unbroken Chain: Opposition to Chain Stores During the Great Depression" (M.A. thesis, University of Wisconsin, Madison, 1985); Thomas W. Ross, *Store Wars: The Chain Tax Movement*, Working Paper No. 34, University of Chicago Center for the Study of the Economy and the State (July 1984); Thomas Ross, "Store Wars: The Chain Tax Movement," *Journal of Law and Economics* 24 (April 1986): 125-37; F. J. Harper, "'A New Battle on Evolution': The Anti-chain Store Trade-at-Home Agitation of 1929- 1930," *American Studies* 16, no. 3 (1982): 407-26; F. J. Harper, "The Anti-chain Store Movement in the United States, 1927-1940" (Ph.D. dissertation, University of Warwick, Centre for the Study of Social History, 1981). For the chains' reply, see E. C. Buehler, *Debate Handbook on the Chain Store Question* (Warren, Kansas: University of Kansas).

For working conditions and management strategies at Woolworth's in the 1930s, Therese Mitchell's *Consider the Woolworth Workers* (New York: League of Women Shoppers, 1940) provides a gold mine of interviews and information, with information on New York organizing as well. Mary Elizabeth Pidgeon's *Women in 5-and-10-Cent Stores and Limited Price Chain Department Stores* (Washington, D.C.: Government Printing Office, 1930; U.S. Department of Labor Women's Bureau Bulletin No. 76) offers a national survey of Woolworth's workers; see also Janet Hooks, *Women's Occupations through Seven Decades* (Washington, D.C.: Government Printing Office, 1947; U.S. Department of Labor Women's Bureau Bulletin No. 218). For tidbits on Woolworth's management strategies see also Baxter, *Chain Store Distribution and Management*, and Walter S. Hayward and Percival White, *Chain Stores: Their Management and Operation*, third ed. (New York: McGraw-Hill, 1928).

For the big picture of the CIO in the 1930s, consult Robert Zieger, *The CIO 1935–1955* (Chapel Hill, N.C.: University of North Carolina Press, 1995); Foster Rhea Dulles and Melvyn Dubofsky, *Labor in America: A History*, fourth ed. (Arlington Heights, Ill.: Harlan Davidson, 1984). For the General Motors strike, the definitive study is Sidney Fine's *Sit-Down: The General Motors Strike of 1936-1937* (Ann Arbor: University of Michigan Press, 1969). For the UAW and the strike, see Nelson Lichtenstein, *The Most Dangerous Man in Detroit: Walter Reuther and the Fate of American Labor* (New York: Basic Books, 1995); Henry Kraus, *Heroes of Unwritten Story: The UAW 1934-39* (Urbana, Ill.: University of Illinois Press, 1993); Edward Levinson, *Labor on the March* (New York: Harper & Bros., 1938).

On the Detroit labor movement in 1937, I am indebted to Steve Babson,

Working Detroit: The Making of a Union Town, with Ron Alpern, Dave Elsila, and John Revitte (New York: Adama Books, 1984); Alpern, Babson, Elsila, and Revitte, *Union Town: A Labor History Guide to Detroit* (Detroit: Workers' Education Local 189); Carlos A. Schwantes, "We've Got 'Em on the Run, Brothers: The 1937 Non-Automotive Sit Down Strikes in Detroit," *Michigan History* (fall 1992): 179-99.

For an understanding of the AFL and women workers, see Alice Kessler-Harris, *Out to Work: A History of Wage-Earning Women in the United States* (New York: Oxford, 1982); Dorothy Sue Cobble, *Dishing It Out: Waitresses and Their Unions in the Twentieth Century* (Urbana, Ill.: University of Illinois Press, 1991); Elizabeth Faue, *Community of Suffering and Struggle: Women, Men, and the Labor Movement in Minneapolis, 1915–1945* (Chapel Hill, N.C.: University of North Carolina Press, 1991); Annelise Orleck, *Common Sense and a Little Fire: Women and Working-Class Politics in the United States, 1900–1965* (Chapel Hill, N.C.: University of North Carolina Press, 1995). For the CIO, see Ruth Milkman, *Gender at Work: The Dynamics of Job Segregation by Sex During World War II* (Urbana, Ill.: University of Illinois Press, 1987); Nancy Gabin, *Feminism in the Labor Movement: Women and the United Auto Workers, 1935-1975* (Ithaca, N.Y.: Cornell University Press, 1990); Vicki Ruiz, *Cannery Women, Cannery Lives: Mexican Women, Unionization, and the California Food Processing Industry*, 1930-1950 (Albuquerque, N. M.: University of New Mexico Press, 1987); Sharon Hartman Strom, "Challenging 'Woman's Place': Feminism, the Left, and Industrial Unionism in the 1930s," *Feminist Studies* 9 (1983): 359-86. For an analysis of the concept of "girl strikers" and their relationship to consumer culture in an earlier period, see Nan Enstad, "Fashioning Political Identities: Cultural Studies and the Historical Construction of Political Subjects," *American Quarterly* 50, no. 4 (1988).

For the Woolworth's strike itself (including many of the headlines employed in my text), I used, first of all, newspaper and magazine accounts of the time, including the *Detroit News, Detroit Times, Detroit Free Press, Chicago Tribune, New York Times, Daily Worker, Women's Wear Daily*, and *Life*. A spectacular set of photographs of the strike is available in the *Detroit News* Collection, Archives of Labor and Urban Affairs, Walter Reuther Library, Wayne State University, Detroit. Two newsreels produced by Pathé News are available through the Grinberg Film Library in New York City. The *Detroit Labor News*, collected in the Archives of Labor and Urban Affairs, Walter Reuther Library, Wayne State University, Detroit, covered the upsurge in Detroit labor activity before, during, and after the strike. Candy Landers of HERE Local 24 (formerly Local 705) generously allowed me to use the local's private papers, including the *Michigan Hotel, Bar, and Restau-*

rant Review, scrapbooks, and Floyd Loew's invaluable correspondence. I was able to find membership lists and a variety of background materials on microfilm at the international offices of HERE in Washington, D.C. I also found material on the strike in *Catering Industry Employee,* HERE's magazine, and in *Retail Clerks International Advocate,* both of which are important sources on their respective unions' activities in 1937. For background, consult especially Cobble, *Dishing It Out;* Matthew Josephson, *Union House, Union Bar: A History of the Hotel and Restaurant Employees and Bartenders International Union, AFL-CIO* (New York: Random House, 1956); and George C. Kirstein, *Stores and Unions: A Story of the Growth of Unionism in Dry Goods and Department Stores.* National statistics on the CIO are from Leo Troy, Trade Union Membership, 1897-1962 (New York: National Bureau of Economic Research, 1995).

For Myra Wolfgang/Mira Komaroff, see Jean Maddern Pitrone, *Myra: The Life and Times of Myra Wolfgang, Trade-Union Leader* (Wyandotte, Mich.: Calibre Books, 1980); Bernard Rosenberg and Saul Weinman, "Young Women Who Work: An Interview with Myra Wolfgang," *Dissent* 19, no. 1 (winter 1972): 29-36; and extensive clippings, resumés, and correspondence in the papers of Local 24, which also provided material on Louis Koenig.

For solidarity with Detroit workers on the part of the retail clerks' union in New York City, as well as its own activities, see materials in the Robert F. Wagner Archives, New York University, including interviews with Clarina Michelson and May Brooks and files on retail clerks' organizing. The Library of Congress collection of the *New York World Telegram* and *Sun* contains photographs of the New York Woolworth's strike, filed under "Labor–Retail" and "Labor-Strikes." *The Retail Employee,* from the New York local that split off from the Retail Clerks' International Protective Association, also reports on organizing activities. For New York union organizing and the national ripple effects of the Detroit strike, see Kirstein, *Stores and Unions,* and the *Retail Clerks International Advocate* throughout 1937 and 1938.

Finally, on the popular culture front, "Chain Store Daisy" is from Harold Rome's *Pins and Needles* (New York: Florence Music, 1937). For text and an analysis of its context, see Michael Denning, *The Cultural Front: The Labor of American Culture in the Twentieth Century* (London and New York: Verso, 1996). *The Devil and Miss Jones* (Republic Entertainment, 1941) is available on video through Republic Entertainment, Inc.

Acknowledgments

I want to express my deepest gratitude to Haymarket Books for this new edition. It's a great honor. Thanks to Anthony Arnove, Julie Fain, and Eric Kerl, for their visible and invisible labors. My special thanks to Todd Chretien for paving the way, for the interview, and for helping connect the dots of my multiple identities. My great thanks also to the glorious Beacon Press and Gayatri Padniak for so generously releasing the rights.

As this edition was being produced, my grand teacher David Montgomery left us. Dedicating this to him doesn't begin to express my debt or capture the magnificent gift of his vision. I hope his spirit lives on in these pages, as it lives on in the movement.

From the Beacon edition:

A great array of people helped me track down sources, understand Detroit in the 1930s, and find people to interview, and I want to thank them all, beginning with Eric Abrahamson, Ron Alpern, Alberta Asmer, Steve Babson, Irwin Bauer, Paul Buhle, Carolyn Davis, Michael Denning, Sean Ellis, Peter Gottlieb, Douglas Haller, Darran Hendricks, Desma Holcomb, Mildred Jeffreys, Bill Mazey, Harry Miller, Kathy Moran, Keith Phelps, Franklin Rosemont, Ethel Schwartz, and Ferrer Valle. Thanks especially to Paul Domeney, Mary Davis, and Ceil McDougle, for their stories of the strike itself and of working at Woolworth's. Thanks to Michael Rogin for sharing his own work on *The Devil and Miss Jones*. My great thanks, as always, to David Montgomery, for help with sources and ongoing inspiration.

I am especially indebted to the Hotel Employees and Restaurant Employees' International Union (HERE) for so generously and with such enjoyable comradeship opening its archives to me, both in Washington, D.C., and in Detroit. Thanks to the people who made it possible: Rick Faith, Pat Lamborn, Candy Landers, Morty Miller, Lee Strieb, and John Wilhelm.

Too late, I want to thank Debra Bernhardt, to whose memory this book is dedicated. Debra was a spectacular fighter for labor history who for almost twenty years guided me to sources in the Wagner Archives at New York University—including all the materials here on retail clerks in New York. Thanks also to the staff of the Wagner Archives; to the staff of the Walter Reuther Library, Wayne State University, especially Tom Featherstone; and to the Grinberg Film Library. I was able to visit all these archives thanks to funding from the UCSC Academic Senate Committee on Research. My astounded thanks, still, to Frank Gravier for tracking down the Pathé Newsreels.

On the home front (and beyond), my deepest thanks to the Usual Suspects for all their support: Barbara Bair, Frank Bardacke, Cathy Buller, Nancy Chen, Sami Chen, Joan Couse, Gerri Dayharsh, Eleanor Engstrand, Julie Greene, Lisbeth Haas, Hamsa Heinrich, Ramona Dayharsh McCabe, Rebecca Dayharsh McCabe, Steve McCabe, Gwendolyn Mink, Amy Newell, Mary Beth Pudup, Gerda Ray, Karin Stallard, Tyler Stovall and Deborah Turner. Thanks to my family—Carolyn, Joseph, and Laura Frank—for their ongoing love and support. (Thanks especially to my mom for finding me an actual Detroit Woolworth's worker, at the San Luis Obispo, California, League of Women Voters.) My particular thanks to the friends who read the manuscript and helped it along with enthusiasm and advice: Miriam Frank (no relation!), Marge Frantz, Desma Holcomb, Ann E. Kingsolver, Greta Schiller, Debbie Shayne, Vanessa Tait, and Andrea Weiss. My special thanks, once again, to Nelson Lichtenstein for his ongoing enthusiasm for my work, for his expertise on Detroit in the 1930s, and for his gracious humor about my pilgrimage to UAW-centrism. Special thanks to Carter Wilson for comradeship in writing, for oh-so-smart advice on the manuscript, and, most important, for enduring (half) the TV movie with Farrah Fawcett as Barbara Hutton.

Thanks, finally, to Robin D. G. Kelley and Howard Zinn for the enormous honor of sharing their marquee, and for the great pleasure of working with them. Thanks to Edna Chiang at Beacon Press for support during the hard parts, and to all the Beacon folks. And, most of all, thanks to Deborah Chasman, who thought up the book and invited me in; who once again gave me great advice; and who was always supportive, savvy, and fun along the way—the editor all writers dream of.

About the author

Dana Frank is professor of History at the University of California, Santa Cruz, and the founder and former Director of the UCSC Center for Labor Studies. Her books include *The Long Honduran Night* (Haymarket, 2018); *Bananeras: Women Transforming the Banana Unions of Latin America* (South End, 2005); *Buy American: The Untold Story of Economic Nation-alism* (Beacon, 1999); *Purchasing Power: Consumer Organizing, Gender, and the Seattle Labor Movement, 1919-1929* (Cambridge, 1994); *Local Girl Makes History: Exploring Northern California's Kitsch Monuments* (City Lights, 2007); and, with Robin D. G. Kelley and Howard Zinn, *Three Strikes: Miners, Musicians, Salesgirls, and the Fighting Spirit of Labor's Last Century* (Beacon, 2001). She is currently writing a book about the AFL-CIO's Cold War in Honduras, to be published by The New Press. She is a member of the American Federation of Teachers Local 2199 and the UCSC Faculty Association and has long been active in labor solidarity work in the U.S. and Honduras. Since the 2009 military coup, she has spoken and written widely on contemporary Honduras for a range of media, including the *New York Times, San Francisco Chronicle, ChicagoTri-bune.com, Progressive.com, CommonDreams.com, NPR, BBC World News, Free Speech Radio News, Al Jazeera English TV, TeleSURTV*, and serves as *The Nation's* correspondent on Honduras.

About Haymarket Books

Haymarket Books is a radical, independent, nonprofit book publisher based in Chicago. Our mission is to publish books that contribute to struggles for social and economic justice. We strive to make our books a vibrant and organic part of social movements and the education and development of a critical, engaged, international left.

We take inspiration and courage from our namesakes, the Haymarket martyrs, who gave their lives fighting for a better world. Their 1886 struggle for the eight-hour day—which gave us May Day, the international workers' holiday—reminds workers around the world that ordinary people can organize and struggle for their own liberation. These struggles continue today across the globe—struggles against oppression, exploitation, poverty, and war.

Since our founding in 2001, Haymarket Books has published more than five hundred titles. Radically independent, we seek to drive a wedge into the risk-averse world of corporate book publishing. Our authors include Noam Chomsky, Arundhati Roy, Rebecca Solnit, Angela Y. Davis, Howard Zinn, Amy Goodman, Wallace Shawn, Mike Davis, Winona LaDuke, Ilan Pappé, Richard Wolff, Dave Zirin, Keeanga-Yamahtta Taylor, Nick Turse, Dahr Jamail, David Barsamian, Elizabeth Laird, Amira Hass, Mark Steel, Avi Lewis, Naomi Klein, and Neil Davidson. We are also the trade publishers of the acclaimed Historical Materialism Book Series and of Dispatch Books.

CPSIA information can be obtained
at www.ICGtesting.com
Printed in the USA
JSHW030347060221
11615JS00003B/55

9 781608 462452